Posted in the Past
Second Delivery

Revealing more true stories
written on a postcard

By

Helen Baggott

First published 2021

Stourcastle Books
www.stourcastle.co.uk

© Helen Baggott

British Library Cataloguing in Publication Data.
A catalogue record for this book is available from the British Library.

ISBN 978-1-9161070-1-4
Printed in Great Britain

Take great care of these people,
their lives were as precious to them as yours is to you.

Contents

Introduction

When I published the first book in this series, *Posted in the Past*, it was the culmination of a project that began 20 or so years earlier. My parents had bought two postcards at a car boot sale and I decided to research the recipients – a mother and her son. I dipped in and out of that research over the years that followed and even visited towns and villages where the family lived. Eventually I was able to pass on my research to family members on both sides of the Atlantic.

It was such a satisfying project that I sought out new postcards to research and those became the book that was published in 2019. I always intended to write more books in this series and *Hands Across the Sea* will explore the journeys of those who emigrated from the UK or enjoyed the pleasure of holidays in the UK and further afield – and, of course, sent home postcards.

As an amateur genealogist, I have used the online tools available to research the people who received the postcards. Most were sent in the early 1900s and I began with the census returns for 1901 and 1911. The 1911 census is particularly useful as it was completed by the head of the household and lists additional information not found in the earlier returns – number of years married, number of children born and of those, the number that had died. All of the family trees I created during the research are available on Ancestry. If you have a particular interest in a family, please contact me and I will provide you with as much information as I can. The trees are set to private so I have some control over who views them. It wasn't necessary for me to bring the trees into a more recent stage than the early 20th century. I wanted an insight into the lives and times of those associated with the postcards and the privacy of all the families in the 21st century is protected. Unless a reader has information about the most recent generations, a connection cannot be easily made.

Genealogy is a fascinating hobby and you may already have researched your own family's past. If you have, you will know that your work is never finished. There's always more to discover and that is certainly true of the families I have researched. However, I have had to find a happy medium between telling the story behind a postcard and tracing the family back to the beginning of available records – as interesting as that would be, the connection with the postcard would be lost. Genealogy provided the tools, but the content is not about just that subject. Sometimes I came across information from a research perspective that needed to be included – problems encountered, inconsistencies with the information available, etc. Beginner genealogists might be encouraged to learn of the problems we all encounter.

By creating a family tree for each postcard, I have been able to place the members of a family into a context suggested by the messages – references to cousins, aunties, brothers become more than words when we know their names and where they lived. Also, many people, including my own relatives, were never known by their registered names; the postcards allow us to meet these people and address them as their friends and relatives might.

If you have watched *Who Do You Think You Are?* and *A House Through Time* you will be familiar with the documents I have used – although I have not included copies here.

Posted in the Past – Second Delivery has been a wonderful project to complete. Even during its writing, I received messages about the families I was researching. Although the trees are not accessible without my permission, the content does appear in searches on Ancestry. As I'm sure any researcher will confirm, sharing the information is as important as undertaking the research in the first place.

The postcards were chosen at random – provided I could read the details, they had a chance of being included.

Many of the families I researched for the first book had members who emigrated to America and Canada. Millions left the UK in the early 1900s to escape rising unemployment and the pollution created as a by-product of the Industrial Revolution. Because of that strong connection on both sides of the Atlantic I decided to look for cards that were also sent from America – either to addresses in the UK or in America.

The four hundredth anniversary of the sailing of the *Mayflower* was celebrated in 2020 and, later, their first Thanksgiving.

Postcards that illustrate the story of the *Mayflower* and beyond have led to finding connections to the American War of Independence and Civil War. Some of these postcards are grouped together in *The Mayflower Connection* – a section dedicated to the story from sailing from Holland, to the United Kingdom, and then on to the New World. This collection begins on page 139.

The Mayflower Connection isn't the only theme followed. Some cards reveal the pain of divorce, celebrated artists, through to the care of sick children.

Despite enhancements, some postcards remain hard to read when reproduced here. Many were written in either a light ink or pencil. However, they are all included (in colour) on a blog that accompanies this book. You will find more information about this in the About the Author section.

It's important to remember that all the postcards belong to a family. When I looked at the census returns – especially for 1911 – it was sobering to discover the deaths of children and young adults. Of course, everyone connected with the actual postcards will not be alive today. When I worked through a postcard's story, it was sometimes a relatively easy process, but taking a moment to remember those lives, and deaths, is important.

At a talk given in 2019, it was commented that my research had been undertaken and shared in a sympathetic manner and I hope I have continued that here in this new book. As I was midway with my research into *Second Delivery*, I received an email from someone who had enjoyed the first book. A genealogist who began in the 1970s, she knew of the work involved and she shared a quote she had come across:

Take great care of these people, their lives were as precious to them as yours is to you.

We live in a world where a message can be written and read by the recipient within seconds. We send postcards today almost as a joke – knowing we could post a message on Facebook before a stamp was fixed. I do hope you enjoy reading these true stories, written on a postcard – and remember those precious lives.

Posted in the
Past
Second Delivery

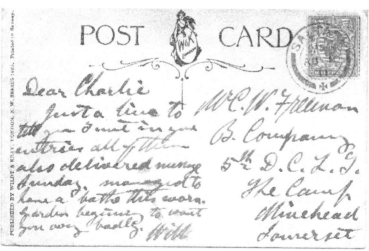

Saltash

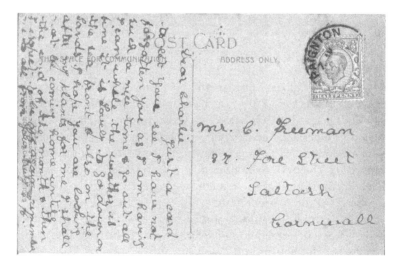

Paignton Pier and Lawns

001231
10 August 1911
Mr CW Freeman
B Company
5th Duke of Cornwall's Light Infantry
The Camp
Minehead
Somerset
Dear Charlie
Just a line to tell you I sent in your entries, all of them. Also delivered nursery's Sunday. Managed to have a bathe this morn. Garden beginning to want you very badly. Will.
Saltash

Mr C Freeman
87 Fore Street
Saltash
Cornwall
Dear Charlie
Just a card to let you see I have not forgotten you as I am having such a nice time and go out all I can while the weather is fine it is lovely to go down on the sea front and also on the sands. I hope you are looking after my plants for me. I shall not be coming home until the end of the month and then I expect to be off again. Remember me to all from yours truly EH.

When I was writing *Posted in the Past*, I knew that I would have to begin the stories with that of Gilbert Freeman and his family. His postcard, sent to him at the Chelsea Barracks in 1913, was bought by my parents with another that was sent to his mother who lived at the time the postcard was sent in Stonehouse, Gloucestershire. Gilbert, I discovered, had been killed in the Battle of the Somme. He has no known grave and his name is recorded on the memorial at Thiepval. As important as it is to remember and acknowledge a soldier's death, it's critical to remember also their shortened life – the life they sacrificed for future generations.

Gilbert was born in Freshford, Somerset in 1894. His father ran the mill in the village. Later, Gilbert would move to Saltash in Cornwall along with some of his siblings. His half-brother, William, ran a shop in Fore Street as a nurseryman and seedsman. On a visit to Saltash's heritage centre I was shown a photograph of William as a relatively young man, standing outside his shop. In the shop's windows can be seen fresh fruit, cut flowers and rosettes. The business was successful and another photograph showed his then widow in the 1960s outside a larger shop, still in Fore Street. The business developed further into selling hardware and continued trading into the early years of the

21st century.

The story of Gilbert and his family connected to his brothers' descendants in America and the UK. Charles and Vincent had emigrated to America – before and after the First World War.

In September 2019 I was booked to give a talk about *Posted in the Past* to Minehead's U3A group. I like to share a postcard of the locations I visit and needed one of Minehead. An online search found the one that illustrates this story. My first reaction was that I had searched for Saltash and not Minehead – until I read the message and the recipient's details.

Charles Freeman (b.1890), who received the postcard that begins this story, had served with the Duke of Cornwall's Light Infantry – in a group photograph sent to me by the UK branch of the family he can be seen wearing their uniform. The message adds so much colour to the research I'd already completed. I knew William's business in Saltash sold fresh produce from the photograph. Could the rosettes on display have been won at the event he mentions?

Charles' postcard was for sale in America and I'll never know why or how it came to be for sale. Of course, I had to buy it. The seller had another postcard that Charles must have taken with him to America. I'm still working on tracing the sender but it's lovely to think that he took this card – and William's – with him.

I shared these new postcards with the UK branch of the family and they told me a lovely story. Charles had intended emigrating to Australia. However, when he found there were no ships sailing there for some time, he decided to go to America. He eventually settled in Massachusetts, followed later by his brother, Vincent.

My focus in the first round of research had been Gilbert, now I had Charles to look at in more detail and of course that took me on another journey. Charles married Mabel Simmonds in America in 1914. In 1911 she was working as a maid for a solicitor in Saltash. I'm told that the couple were engaged before he left for America. I wonder what she thought about his change of plans?

Mabel was born in Devon in 1892. She was the daughter of a sailor, Daniel Simmonds. I'm always delighted, though not necessarily surprised, at the wonderful coincidences postcards reveal and this one is no exception. Daniel was born in Sherborne, Dorset in 1840 – ten minutes from where I live. I haven't managed to trace the actual houses he lived in, but I have walked along the streets.

Mabel's brother, Alfred, was killed in 1914. He was a sailor and aboard HMS *Amphion* – the first ship of the Royal Navy to be sunk in the First World War.

As I was adding the finishing touches to this story, I was contacted by Mucknell Abbey in Worcestershire about one of Gilbert and Charles' sisters.

Dora had sent the postcard to Mrs Freeman in Stonehouse (the second postcard bought by my parents). I already knew that she had never married and is recorded in several documents as a teacher. She actually, I was told, became an Anglican nun. I was delighted to pass on information that would be used in her necrology and be read out on the anniversary of her death each year. Dora had been with the Order in Burford Priory, Oxfordshire – built on the site of a 13th-century Augustinian hospital, and later a home visited by James I who stayed there for three nights in 1603. From 1949 Burford Priory housed The Society of the Salutation of Our Lady and almost 60 years later the community sold the property and it is now a private home.

Researching a family tree can never be considered 'finished' and I am sure I will return to the Freeman family in the future. In 2020 I was contacted by a teacher at Freshford school in Somerset – the village where Gilbert and his siblings grew up. I was so pleased to share more information with her about the Freemans – knowing that Gilbert's short life will be remembered by the children of the village.

During the first 100 years of census-taking, the population of England and Wales grew more than threefold, to around 32 million and a further 4.5 million or so in Scotland—The National Archives

Unknown Warrior's Grave, Westminster Abbey, London

002351
19 May 1926
Mrs Butlin
Railway Cottage
Sandridge
Nr St Albans
Herts
Dear Ellen
If fine, all come down tomorrow Thursday about 12:30.
Love Bessie

In 1887, George Butlin and Ellen née Wheeler, the daughter of a farm bailiff, lived in Worksop, Nottinghamshire where their first son, James, was born.

George Butlin spent all his recorded working life on the railways. He was born in Coln St Aldwyns, Gloucestershire in 1863 and appears in various records as a signalman.

By 1889 they had moved to Sandridge, Hertfordshire where their other children – Sylvia, George, Charles, Marjorie and Muriel – were born.

James served in the First World War in the Pay Corps where he became a sergeant. In 1917 he married Minnie Slough, whose father also worked on the railways. The couple eventually emigrated to Canada and lived in New Denver, British Columbia – where Minnie died in 1926.

Marjorie and Muriel appear in several passenger lists travelling to and from Canada and Marjorie died in New Denver in 1987. James outlived his siblings by many years and died aged 107, also in New Denver.

Before the war, the youngest brother, Charles, was an engineer. He died in 1915 and is buried at St Lawrence's church, Stratford-sub-Castle in Wiltshire. There are 47 war graves in the churchyard and the church's website provides this information about Charles:

Sapper 56987, Royal Engineers, UK
Died of Cerebro Spinal Fever at the Isolation Hospital on 16.3.15 age 20
Stationed at Sutton Veny

Charles' burial records reveal that he died at the isolation hospital in Stratford-sub-Castle – as did all but one of the other entries on his page.

I found more information about Charles and his death on a wonderful website: www.WiltshireAtWar – one of those great community initiatives that have commemorated and remembered the war.

A volunteer had photographed the headstones and Charles' carries this inscription:

56987 SAPPER
CHARLES R. BUTLIN
ROYAL ENGINEERS
16TH MARCH 1915 AGE 20
ALSO IN LOVING MEMORY OF
JAMES WHEELER BUTLIN
21ST JANUARY 1995 AGE 107

This additional information is from the website:

The 'R' in Charles R. Butlin stands for Reginald, and he and James were sons of George and Ellen Butlin, of Sandridge, St Albans, Herts. Charles was a member of the 108th Field Company, and was stationed at Sutton Veny when he died of Cerebro Spinal Fever at the Isolation Hospital, Stratford-sub-Castle.
Salisbury Isolation Hospital at Stratford-sub-Castle was built in 1911 and stayed a hospital until 1951. It was situated on The Portway close to Old Sarum Airfield.

I'm sure there must be others, but this is the only headstone I've seen that has an inscription added so many years later.

In the UK, the surname Butlin is best known perhaps for Billy Butlin – Sir William Heygate Edmund Colborne Butlin MBE – who created the network of holiday camps and revolutionised how families holidayed from the 1950s into the 21st century. Billy was born in South Africa and his parents married in Gloucestershire in a small village about 25 miles from where George Butlin had been born in 1863. Could there be a connection? Perhaps – but not close enough!

BENEATH THIS STONE RESTS THE BODY
OF A BRITISH WARRIOR
UNKNOWN BY NAME OR RANK
BROUGHT FROM FRANCE TO LIE AMONG
THE MOST ILLUSTRIOUS OF THE LAND
AND BURIED HERE ON ARMISTICE DAY
11 NOV: 1920, IN THE PRESENCE OF
HIS MAJESTY KING GEORGE V
HIS MINISTERS OF STATE
THE CHIEFS OF HIS FORCES
AND A VAST CONCOURSE OF THE NATION
THUS ARE COMMEMORATED THE MANY
MULTITUDES WHO DURING THE GREAT
WAR OF 1914–1918 GAVE THE MOST THAT
MAN CAN GIVE LIFE ITSELF
FOR GOD
FOR KING AND COUNTRY
FOR LOVED ONES HOME AND EMPIRE
FOR THE SACRED CAUSE OF JUSTICE AND
THE FREEDOM OF THE WORLD
THEY BURIED HIM AMONG THE KINGS BECAUSE HE
HAD DONE GOOD TOWARD GOD AND TOWARD
HIS HOUSE

Barron Falls, Queensland, Australia

00347
27 November 1911
Miss AF White
15 Fulham Palace Road
London
England
I hope you received our parcel safely and that you are not in the hands of the doctor after your Christmas feasts.
We are having terrible weather, it has been trying to rain for a fortnight and it is very hot and muggy and everything is scortched [sic] and dried up.
With best wishes
This view is in North Q'land.

Annie White lived with her two sisters, Louisa and Mary. Annie was a pianoforte teacher and their father, John White, was a pianoforte-maker. She was born in London in 1867 and at the age of 47 she married Edgar Nodes, an undertaker some 12 years her junior.

Edgar appears in Australian electoral rolls in 1913 showing that he lived in Kangaroo Point, Oxley, Queensland. He returned to England in June 1914 and married Annie two weeks later. The marriage register was very useful in showing Edgar's distinctive 'E' – used to sign his name – which perfectly matched the 'E' of England on the postcard. The register shows that Edgar's father, Walter Nodes (b.1854), was also an undertaker and in at least one census return he is shown as both an undertaker and coffin-maker.

Edgar had at least four brothers. Walter (b.1876) emigrated to America around 1895, and lived with his American wife Margaret and their children in New York.

Frederick became a bookseller's assistant and died in 1908.

Arnold was a clerk. His son, Peter Nodes (b.1921), was killed in the Second World War and is one 20,000 names remembered on the Air Forces Memorial at Runnymede.

Edgar, who sent the postcard, served in the First World War, as did another brother, Percy – also an undertaker. He was killed in 1917 and his name is listed at the memorial at Tyne Cot in Belgium as another victim who has no known grave.

The Nodes were a family of undertakers. It's possible to trace many branches from Edgar's grandfather, John Nodes (b.1814), that have links to this profession. Edgar's uncle John Nodes – his father's brother – became head of a business that still trades today with many branches throughout London (in recent years it has become part of a larger company but retains the name John Nodes Funeral Service).

In 1920, Edgar's cousin Horace Nodes was asked by the UK government to create a coffin for an unidentified British soldier. Horace was president of the British Undertakers' Association and decided 'that the burden of payment for the coffin should not be met by the general public' and asked each member of the association to donate one shilling. One week later, Horace accompanied the coffin to France where the soldier's remains were placed inside and brought back to Britain, ultimately to rest in Westminster Abbey.

I can say with certainty that every family I have researched would have been affected by the First World War – either directly or indirectly. Many of the casualties have no known graves – including Gilbert Freeman whose postcard began this project. That Horace's cousin lost his life and also has no known grave makes this particular story very poignant. My research began with three spinsters living in London. The story of Annie White and her husband Edgar Nodes and his family opened up more information about the effect of the First World War and the memorials that are still honoured around the world – and in Westminster Abbey in London.

Horace Nodes would later remember the events that led to the bringing home of the Unknown Warrior.

There was a real thrill, he recalled, as he and his colleagues awaited the arrival before they embarked HMS *Verdun*.

Hours later the ship arrived at Dover where a band played Land of Hope and Glory – *The thrill of it sent shivers down my back and I was proud to be British.*

In November 2020, The Western Front Association produced a special edition of their magazine *Stand To!* that shared the story of the Unknown Warrior and of how other countries brought their own Warriors home.

If you have an interest in this aspect of our history, I do recommend you join the Association.

Guelph, Ontario

004386
18 September 1911
Mrs Little
Little Coxwell
Faringdon
Berkshire
England
This is a view of the town I am living in just now – or rather we look down on it from the hill top. I hope you and Mr Little are well. I have not heard anything of you for such a long time.
MAG Waller

Charles Little (b.1827) and Amy née Griffin (b.1833) were born in the neighbouring villages of Little Coxwell and Great Coxwell. The 1911 census reveals that they had two children and one child, Mary, had died. Living with them at the time of the census was their surviving daughter, who was married, Sarah (b.1855) and a great-grandson, Arthur Rowley, who was born in West Bromwich in 1901. Interestingly, Charles and Amy didn't marry until 1859.

Sarah married local man Edward Miles and the couple had three children, including a daughter, Amy, who was born in 1875. By 1881 they had moved to West Bromwich where Edward was a railway employee.

Amy married Staffordshire-born Arthur Rowley and together they had four children, including young Arthur who was with his great-grandparents in 1911. At this time, Amy and Arthur were with her father, Edward, in Smethwick. They lived in Spon Lane, an area known for the manufacture of glass which ties in with Arthur's job as a labourer in a glass factory. Young Arthur returned to the Midlands and in 1939 worked as a motor driver, living in Spon Lane with his parents and siblings.

Who was MAG Waller?

In 1901, Margaret Arabella Glascott Waller lived with her parents in Little Coxwell. Charles Waller was a vicar, born in Staffordshire in 1841, and he married Arabella Stubbs in 1865. Like Charles' father, Arabella's was also a vicar and she was born in Ireland in 1832. The couple had eight children and Margaret was the youngest, born in 1876 in Hampstead, London.

The 1911 census provides information about some of Margaret's siblings: Lucy – organist at the parish church in Great Coxwell; Herbert – doctor in Kings Norton, Worcestershire (later, in Wooburn, Buckinghamshire); Alfred – vicar in Chester. From other records I found that Edward, another brother, also became a vicar and eventually Bishop of Madras, India.

Margaret, who sent the postcard, appears in the 1911 census return in London, Ontario living with another brother, Charles, also a vicar. Charles married twice and died in Ontario in 1944.

Although it's not clear when she returned to England, Margaret died in Sussex.

Given that there was more than a generation between Margaret and Amy, to whom she sent the postcard, it's touching to read such a lovely message sent to people she was clearly fond of. It's possible that they died before Margaret returned – but perhaps Lucy played the organ at Charles Little's funeral in 1913. Amy died ten years later in Staffordshire.

England and Wales census dates
(for more information about Scotland and other UK areas go to
The National Archives or your genealogical research provider)

1841 – 6 June

1851 – 30 March

1861 – 7 April

1871 – 2 April

1881 – 3 April

1891 – 5 April

1901 – 31 March

1911 – 2 April

1939 – 29 September (register)

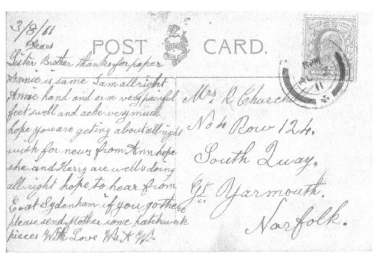

SS *Linnet*, Crinan Canal, Ardrishaig

005205
3 August 1911
Mrs R Churchill
No 4 Row 124
South Quay
Great Yarmouth
Norfolk
Dear Sister Brother
Thanks for paper.
Annie is same. I am all right.
Annie hand and arm very painful feet swell and ache very much.
Hope you are getting about all right.
Wish for news from Ann.
Hope she and Harry are well and doing all right. Hope to hear from E at Sydenham and if you go there please send Mother some patchwork pieces.
With Love

When Matilda Wright and Robert Churchill married in 1860, he is listed as a mariner living at Row 125 and Matilda is at Row 124 – narrow alleys in Great Yarmouth. Both their fathers were master mariners.

Matilda lived at number 4 with her widowed brother, also named Robert. His wife, Maria, had died in 1904 and at that time the couple were at this address.

Brother Robert had completed the 1911 census and included Matilda as a widow who'd had one child who had died – Emily Churchill was born in 1861, a year after Matilda had married.

In two subsequent census returns, Matilda is away from Great Yarmouth, working as a servant in Greenwich and Rotherhithe. Her status is 'married'. More than one online tree gives husband Robert as dying in America in 1929. However, the only evidence to support this is a directory listing for R Churchill – with no confirmation of the first name, age or place of birth. Robert doesn't appear in any census returns in the UK, so perhaps he did leave for America and Matilda assumed the status of a widow. Even with the relatively low number of families I've researched it does seem that many wives hid their possible abandonment behind being a widow.

It's worth mentioning here how important it is to query the details found in other online trees. Without being able to confirm Robert's timeline it was important not to create a new life for him elsewhere. Of course, it might be that the families had additional information that led them to accepting this fact.

Argyle Street, Glasgow

006335
22 July 1911
Mrs G Henbrey
Faraday House
Rye
Sussex
England
Just another view of the city. Hope you are all well. It has been raining here.
Very miserable and quite chilly.
E

Sarah Henbrey née Barnett was the daughter of a farmer of 23 acres, William Barnett. She was born in Ockham, Surrey in 1846 and in 1869 she married George Henbrey, the son of a miller from Playden, Sussex and later lived in the small village of Iden. Their mill appears in a directory of 'lost mills of Sussex'. Unfortunately it's one of a few without extra information.

Sarah and George had five children and by 1911 one had died. Living with them at the time of the census was Elsie Kelly, their married daughter. George added that she had been married for six years. George's employment is recorded as a corn factor agent and a surveyor and sanitary inspector. I found a marriage between Richard Kelley and Elsie Maud Henbrey in 1905 – but could not confirm that our Elsie was Elsie Maud, or that her father had misspelled her married name.

In October 1911 Elsie Henbrey sailed to Canada, destined for Hamilton, Ontario. Her occupation is given as pianist. In 1912, in Hamilton, she married ironworker and rigger Alfred Rayment Martin, who was born in Plaistow, London. The marriage register confirms her parents' details including her father's occupation as surveyor. Alfred was a bachelor at the time of the marriage and Elsie is listed as a spinster. Alfred had emigrated to Canada in 1907 and had served in the navy during the Boer War. In 1918, Elsie married again – this time to a widower, John Severs. Once more she is listed as a spinster. Her parents' details confirm this is our Elsie.

There's much that's confusing about Elsie's story and even checking other online trees didn't help. One had the same basic details as my own – except that Elsie had 11 siblings. I had to discount any new information that researcher had because it was too wide of the mark. The 1911 census isn't always 100 per cent accurate, but it's unlikely George Henbrey made such a major error in counting the number of children he'd had.

Very often we see the marital status in registers and other official records and accept it on face value – Elsie's example proves to be the exception. One bonus of Elsie signing so many marriage registers is that I was able to match her writing to that of the postcard – so at least that was one question solved!

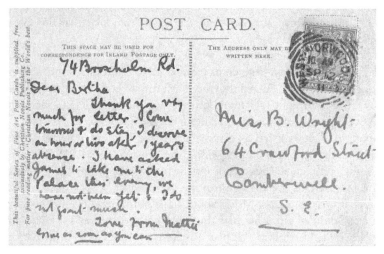

Parish Church, Ilkley

007206
12 September 1911
Miss B Wright
64 Crawford Street
Camberwell
SE
74 Broxholm Road
Dear Bertha
Thank you very much for letter. Come tomorrow and do stay. I deserve an hour or two after
1 year's absence. I have asked James to take me to the Palace this evening. We have not
been yet and I do not go out much.
Love from Mattie
Come as soon as you can.

Emily Bertha Wright was the daughter of Uriah and Emma Wright. In 1911, Uriah was a retired civil servant. Bertha (b.1880) was the youngest of eight children and was a ledger clerk.

Uriah was born in 1841 and in 1861 he was a builder's clerk. Over the years that followed his career developed into a draughtsman, civil servant with the Home Office and an assistant surveyor with the prison commissioner.

I found Mattie as Matilda Livock, wife of James, a bank clerk. Matilda née Graham was born in 1885 in Ham, near Sandwich in Kent. Her father, Alexander Graham, was born in Stirling, Scotland and was a warrant officer in the army. In 1911 the family lived in Norwood – not far from Mattie's address on the card.

In her message, Mattie mentions visiting the Palace. Crystal Palace was not far from their home and in 1911 it hosted the Festival of Empire – a celebration for George V's coronation. It opened in May and ran for several months.

Mattie and James appear in marriage records for 1927 – with new spouses. Mattie married Charles Chilton a farmer – and the couple eventually lived in Oxfordshire. Interestingly, their marriage certificate shows Mattie's status as 'the divorced wife of James Livock'.

James married Margaret Morrison and lived in Paddington – where James had become a bank manager.

Was the message on the postcard tinged with a note of unhappiness and frustration? Perhaps my interpretation is affected by the knowledge that the marriage didn't last.

Port Soderick, Isle of Man

008349
15 September 1911
Miss Ethel Booth
80 Regent Road
Blackpool
Ethel, you or Morris and go and see if ice cream man is on sands tomorrow Saturday and if it's not too late on my arrival I will go and see him I don't mean either of you to go to him.
With Love
Hope Morris is a good boy and doing his practice.
EA Kay

Although it's difficult to transcribe the postcard message completely, it's clear that Esther Kay is discussing ice cream and her son James Morris Kay who was born in 1899. According to the 1911 census, Esther Kay lived at the address on the card with her son and Ethel Booth, a servant. A few weeks later, in April 1911, the mother and child sailed from Liverpool to Boston, Massachusetts for a visit.

On 16 July 1917, a day after his eighteenth birthday, Morris joined the Royal Navy, beginning his service on HMS *President II*. He later transferred to the RAF. His occupation on enlisting is given as a fitter and he later became a mechanic.

In 1898, Esther Morris married Moses Kay. Both were born in Heywood, Lancashire. Apart from their son's baptism records there's very little online that confirms Esther and Moses lived together at the address in Regent Road. However, a substantial document from 1902 does give the address for the couple. Esther petitioned for divorce and the records, that cover a long period of protracted and detailed statements, reveal that the couple had suffered a short and painful marriage.

Moses was accused of multiple instances of adultery with prostitutes and a number of women – including Mrs Hammond, the wife of a company secretary who lived at 41 Regent Road. Mary Hammond was sixteen years older than Moses and she and her husband still lived in Regent Road in 1911. As well as listing the women, the locations of the alleged encounters are also recorded including the Bull's Head in Merton and a temperance hotel.

Moses was also accused of physical abuse and that included, in 1899, 'throwing baby James violently to the foot of their bed… swearing at Esther and beating her'.

It's no surprise to find Esther living with her widowed father, retired pawnbroker James Morris, in 1901. The petition for divorce also included financial details – that Esther's father paid for her and Morris' upkeep and that he also lived at the address in Regent Road. Esther remained in Blackpool until her death and Moses died in Heywood in the 1920s.

Ludgate Hill, London.

POST CARD.

Message (Inland & Foreign Post).
NEW REGULATION.

ADDRESS.

Miss Hilda Ashley
East View
Grange-over-Sands
Wt. Lancs

Ludgate Hill, London

009260
19 June 1910
Miss Hilda Ashley
East View
Grange-over-Sands
Lancashire

Some family trees are full of branches that seem intent on taking you off and away – with baffling coincidences that create errors and confusion. This postcard's tree needed several rounds of pruning before I was able to see the branches for what they were. In 1911 Hilda Ashley lived with her grandmother, Sarah Ann Mossop, and two of Sarah's children, Edith and Harold Ashley, a railway clerk. Sarah was a widow and it was her marriages that created the confusion. I knew from the 1911 census that she was born in Poynton, Cheshire in 1840. The two adult children were born in Lancashire. Hilda was born in 1906 in Harrow, Middlesex.

Working back through Sarah's life via the census returns, I found her in 1901 – as widowed Mrs Mossop – with four of her own children and four stepchildren. This included Frederick Ashley who I would later discover was Hilda's father. In 1881, Sarah is the wife of schoolteacher Thomas Ashley in East Broughton, Lancashire. After his death in 1885, Sarah married widower John Mossop in 1889. Mossop was a grocer and confectioner and in 1891 the family lived in East Broughton – with eight children from their earlier marriages. He died eight years after the marriage and it is his first wife who helped create the confusion others had found with this family and the errors I discovered in other trees. Sarah Ann Holliday was born in 1839 – just a few months before our Sarah Ann. Having the same first and middle name allowed other researchers to merge them as one person – despite Sarah Ann Holliday being born in Cheshire.

Why was young Hilda living with her grandmother? In 1911, her father Frederick appears in Lewisham, living as a married boarder and working as a printer's reader. He is living with Arthur Frankling and his family, who is also a printer's reader. In 1904 Frederick married Annie Smith and the couple had two daughters – Hilda and Annie. In 1911, Annie is living with her mother and maternal grandmother in Rickmansworth, Hertfordshire. In 1939, Annie worked for a tobacconist in Lambeth. At the same time, Hilda still lived in Lancashire. Did the sisters grow up apart from each other and, perhaps, one of their parents? I think so. In 1908, Frederick petitioned for divorce from Annie and named a John Smith as co-respondent. The family must have remained in contact as Annie is mentioned in Frederick's probate records in 1955. By 1939 he had returned to Lancashire. Given that Frederick was living in London for a time, it is likely that he sent Hilda the card which was sent from Catford.

Cocoanut Tree, Florida

Winter Home of John D Rockefeller, Ormond Beach, Florida

Orange Grove in Blossom, Florida

010265
1927
Mrs H Womersley
Ivy House
Crow Edge
Hazlehead
Sheffield
England
This is only short of the monkey to throw the nuts down to us. But there's plenty on the ground
SEH

7 May 1928
Miss Freda Womersley
Greetings from Aunty
XXXXXX

20 May 1928
Miss Freda Womersley
Loving Greetings from Aunty and Hoodlums.
Huggs [sic] *and kisses to my Girley* [sic]

I took a chance with these three cards. They were posted in 1928 – falling between the 1911 census and the 1939 register might have made them impossible to research. However, I found the birth of a Freda Womersley in 1922 and that gave me her mother's maiden name of Battye and then Freda's parents' marriage in 1919. The marriage register confirmed that the couple lived at Crow Edge – proof that I was following the correct family.

In 1911, Freda's father, Henry Womersley, was married to Ann Mitchel. They had had one child who had died. Also listed was John Kaye, their adopted son, born in 1903.

When John Kaye married Alice Dearnley in 1928 the marriage register confirmed that his father was Eli Kaye. John's baptism records revealed that he had a twin brother, Thomas, and his mother's name was Clara. With the full details of his family I found mother Clara née Wortley with Eli and eight children in 1911 in Thurlstone – a few miles from Hazlehead. It was also recorded that they'd had 12 children in total and that two had died. With so many children – all born within a short period of time – perhaps it's understandable (though no less shocking) that John was adopted. The 1911 census confirms that their home had only four rooms.

John's surname was never changed and he certainly knew his father's details for them to be recorded in the marriage register.

In 1915, when John was 12, Ann Womersley died and four years later

Henry married Ellen Battye – Freda's mother.

Henry's father had also married twice. Jeremiah Womersley's first wife was Sarah Kaye and she died in 1872. Jeremiah then married Martha Lindley and the couple had at least two children. Was Eli Kaye a relative of Sarah's? It's certainly possible he was a nephew. Jeremiah had children with both wives and those half-siblings had their own families in the area which was known for its ironworks. The main employer in Crow Edge was the Hepworth Iron Company which worked mines and clay pits.

Jeremiah was a night watchman and Henry was a foreman in an ironworks. Eli was a grinder and John, when he married in 1928, was a public service vehicle driver. His twin brother, Thomas, became a brick-maker. In 1939, Henry is listed as a retired manager of a clay works.

I never traced with any certainty who had sent the postcards from America. Although that's disappointing, I am pleased that it led me to discover the story of John Kaye.

The first adoption legislation was introduced in the UK in 1926. Before this, adoption was organised by charities and societies, and the adoptive parents had few legal rights. In fact, the biological parent could demand custody of their child several years later.

Saint Scholastica's Abbey, Teignmouth

011213
30 January 1905
Mrs Forsman
4 Eleanor Street
Bute Docks
Cardiff
Dear Mrs Forsman
Just a card to let you know I am still alive and kicking, hoping you are all in good health.
Remember me to <u>Tom</u>.
I am yours ac
Ted
<u>*I am not Bill Bailey*</u>

Anna Forsman née Leo was born in Germany in 1859. She married Finland-born ship's carpenter Andreas Gustav Forsman in 1886 in St George's German Lutheran church in Battersea, London.

Andreas became a naturalised citizen in 1914 but doesn't appear in any census returns with his family. However, he does appear in crew lists on ships around the world.

The couple had two children – Gertrude and Gustav – who were born in London. The 1891 census shows Anna and her children living with her widowed mother, Wilhelmina, in West Ham, London.

Gertrude became a cashier in a restaurant and Gustav worked for a draper. In 1909 he married Sarah Whiston, a dressmaker's apprentice. Sarah's family also had seafaring connections. Her father, James, was born in Cheshire in 1841 and served in the Royal Navy and then as a coast guard in Wales. In 1861 he appears as a crew member aboard HMS *Nile*.

Five of Sarah's brothers served in either the Merchant or Royal Navy and three became petty officers.

Did Ted, who sent the postcard, ever return? Won't you come home, Bill Bailey?

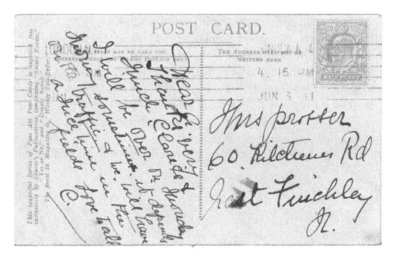

The Ovens River and Mount Feathertop, Australian Alps

012346
3 June 1911
Mrs Prosser
60 Kitchener Road
East Finchley
Dear A
Thanks very much. Clarice and I will be over on Monday morning sometime. It depends on the traffic and we will have a nice time in the fields.
Love to all
C.

Some family trees are so muddled that I'm not sure if even their relatives have found their way along the branches successfully.

This postcard should have been straightforward. The 1911 census return confirmed that Ada (b.1880) lived at the address with her husband, Thomas Prosser, who was a clerk from St Arvans, Wales, and their two children, Avis and Douglas. Also at the address was Louisa Smitheringale, a 15-year-old typist for a grocer whose relationship to the head of the household was sister-in-law – suggesting she was Ada's sister and they shared the same surname. This was confirmed with the marriage records of Thomas and Ada, who married in 1898. Ada was born in Grantham, and Louisa in Marylebone, London.

I found the Smitheringale family in Grantham, Lincolnshire. Louise's father, James, was a general labourer (born in Bourne, Lincolnshire in 1851) and her mother is listed as Marion. She also appears in other records as Mary Ann Saxton. Louise is listed as Janet with the official name of Louise Janet in the birth register. This seemed to be a common theme with this family – using the middle name in some records. It became so baffling that I wondered if two families had been confused. I checked with other online trees and they had the same information – that the Smitheringales had four children – Louisa, Ada, James and Edith Elsie. However, in 1911, James (the father), declares himself as a widower and the father of only two children. Living with him in Grantham is Edith, listed as Elsie.

With online records it's often possible to confirm the real identities of all the close relatives. In this tree, buying the birth certificates of the four children would certainly eliminate all the queries. Just because the information I found was confirmed in the other trees doesn't mean any of them are correct.

As I was tidying my notes and confirming Ada's birth records I found that she was registered in 1881 as Ada Annie Saxton. Her marriage records show her maiden name as Smitheringale. I then realised that her parents, or the couple I had as her parents, hadn't married until 1883. It seems that Mary Ann was unmarried when she had Ada and that Ada was either formally adopted by James or had taken his surname later. I revisited the trees I'd looked at and none of them had this information.

Illegitimate children being accepted into a new family after marriage wasn't necessarily common – but I have come across it before. In my first book I shared the story of an unmarried mother having a child, marrying and having more children, and that first child either taking the husband's name informally or by legal process. After that husband's death the widow lived as mistress to a grocer and had several children with him – the children's surnames covered all permutations, including some with just the grocer's surname (he was a widowed father) and others hyphenated with both surnames. As fascinating as that all sounds, I'm sure neither of the two mothers I've researched had easy lives with their illegitimate children. The facts only tell us that they found partners who were able to accept them – but at what price?

Although it was disappointing not to find the sender of the card in the extended tree, it was interesting to see that more than 100 years ago, visits could be affected by traffic!

The Penny Black was first produced in May 1840 – a few months after the introduction of a standard pre-paid rate of postage for delivery anywhere in Great Britain and Ireland.

Old Toll House, Great Yarmouth

013209
July 1909
Miss Wort
7 Chalk Hill
Bushey
Herts
Dear Ethel
We all have a fine time down here but sorry to say it is very cold. Like the place very much.
Hoping you are all well.
Love…

Ethel Wort was the only child of Edward Wort and Lizzie née Marley. She was born in Balham in 1885 and by 1901 the family had moved to Bushey where Edward was a baker, cook and confectioner.

Edward was born in Bassett, Hampshire. His father was a gardener and in 1871 he declared that Edward was in the Royal Navy and belonged to HMS *Vincent*. Other census returns confirm Edward as being with his family. A naval record of service highlights conflicting information about Edward – giving his date of birth as 28 March 1864 – two years later than estimated from the census and baptism records. Is it the correct Edward? Well, the only ship listed is the *Vincent*. A coincidence? No, I do believe this is the correct Edward – and that a mistake was made. In 1939, Edward's date of birth is given as 1 November 1862 and this agrees with the census returns. It also helps when eliminating the birth records of children with the same name over the two-year period. According to naval records Edward was invalided out.

At the time Edward was attached to the *Vincent*, the masted vessel was primarily used for training. Earlier, the ship was involved in the transportation of troops during the Crimean War.

Ethel's story also creates a puzzle. In 1911 she is a music teacher. Later, there are two Ethel M Worts who married – with husbands Cutchee and Bryant. Without obtaining the marriage certificate of one or both, I wasn't able to confirm who my Ethel had married. Of course, if Ethel had been a relative of mine it's likely I would have known the name and the problem would have been solved within seconds. Looking at the trees available online did not solve the problem – several had listed her as having two husbands. Not impossible, but unlikely – especially as both men are listed with their Ethels in 1939.

This dilemma again highlights the problems of accepting information from online trees. Ethel may have married a lorry driver from Woolwich, or she may have married a dairy farmer from Hertfordshire. I lean towards the farmer – although the jury's out on this.

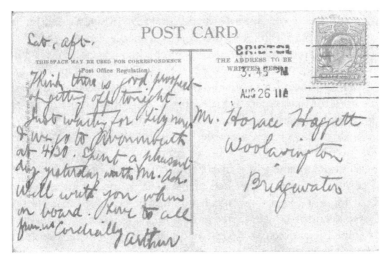

House of Parliament, Westminster, London

014200
26 August 1911
Sat. aft.
Mr Horace Haggett
Woolavington
Somerset
Think there is good possibility of getting off tonight.
Just waiting for Lily now and we go to Avonmouth at 4.30.
Spent a pleasant day yesterday with Mr Ash.
Will write you when on board.
Love to all from us
Cordially Arthur

Horace was born in 1876 and worked as a watchmaker. Although he didn't marry, he had several siblings including Arthur (b.1869) who was a Baptist minister. On the day he sent the postcard, Arthur was about to return to America – he left the same day, sailing aboard the *Royal Edward*. Arthur had arrived in the UK on 5 July 1911, aboard the *Campania*.

His wife was Frances Evans (b.1867) and her family had emigrated from Wales to America where her father was a farmer. Arthur and Frances lived in Hiawatha, Kansas and had at least three children who were born in America.

Arthur was waiting for Lily to arrive, his sister who worked in Bristol. She was born in 1883 and worked as a shopkeeper and postmistress. In 1939, Horace was living with his sister in Bridgwater. In 1911, around the time Arthur was about to sail home via Canada, Lily was a shop assistant in Bristol.

Another sister, Alice, was a dressmaker and in 1901 she lived in Bournemouth, Hampshire (now in Dorset). She married Robert Chamberlain, a shopkeeper from Stroud, Gloucestershire and the couple eventually lived in Margam, Wales where Robert was a grocer.

This wasn't the family's only connection to Wales. Another brother, Hedley, was a butcher in Glamorgan at the time of his death in 1890.

I came across a wonderful photograph of another brother, Francis, who was born in 1867. His occupation is listed as being a shirt and collar-maker. Later, he would become mayor – with Haggett Close named in his honour.

Arthur, who sent the postcard, wasn't the only family member to relocate to America. Wesley, who was born in 1882, appears in Massachusetts in 1910. In 1915, a census return shows him with his wife and children in Salamanca, New York where he worked as a car repairer.

In 1901, Horace was living with his father, George, and his stepmother, Elizabeth. Horace's mother, Anne Smeltzer, had died in 1887. Anne was born in India where her father, Philip Smeltzer, was serving in the army. Her mother was Mary née Andrews and she provides a link to Somerset – she was born in Woolavington.

After Anne's death, Horace's father married Elizabeth Callen née Ash who was a widow. Perhaps this solves the puzzle of who the 'Mr Ash' that Arthur mentions might be. Elizabeth had at least one brother – William. At the time the postcard was sent, William worked as a bootmaker in Bristol – so it's entirely possible he was able to spend some time with Arthur.

Although Arthur signs the postcard with *Love to all from us* I wasn't able to find any other family members aboard the ship.

In 1861, an enumerator in Preston was shocked by the poverty of a neighbourhood in his patch and was at pains to point out one particular aspect of the deprivation he found there: '…namely the serious insufficiency of conveniences for the easement of nature'—The National Archives

The Pier, Cleethorpes

015201
Printed Paper
20 July 1921
Miss C Staples
Linden Lodge
Ashford
Middlesex
Love to all.
Yours
Viv

Mildred Connie Staples was born in 1900 and in 1911 she lived with her family in Ashford. Her father, Arthur Staples, was a wine merchant and the son of gamekeeper Walter Staples. When Walter married Mary Rye in 1847, he is recorded as a blacksmith.

Connie's mother, May née Denison, was the daughter of Charles Denison, a barrister – himself the son of a barrister.

The 1911 census shows that Arthur and May had had five children and that one had died. In addition to Connie, the children that survived were: Arthur Vivian, Olga and Leslie.

Viv served in the First World War with the Royal Artillery. In 1939 he appears as the manager of an off-licence in London, with his wife, Ethel, and their son, James, who was a musician.

Olga married Liverpool postal worker William Fazakerley. His father, Thomas, was a plumber – as was his father, another Thomas.

Leslie married Muriel Tokely and in 1939 the couple lived in Staines, Middlesex where Leslie was a fitter of food processing equipment.

In 1939 Connie is living with her parents, Arthur and May, in Hythe, Kent. Up to this time she had not married.

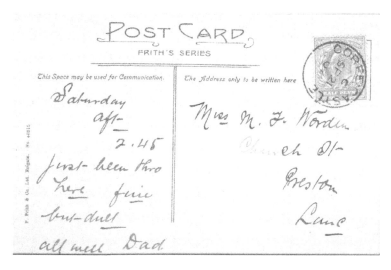

Corfe Castle

016202
21 September 1907
Miss MF Worden
Church Street
Preston
Lancashire
Saturday aft. 2.45
Just been through here. Fine but dull.
All well.
Dad.

Mary Worden was born in Preston in 1885. Her father, William, was a wholesale milliner. In 1901, Mary lived with her parents and two brothers – including Joseph who was a milliner's assistant. William was a relatively successful businessman. His own parents, Henry and Margaret, were also in the same business as tailor/draper and milliner – at Church Street, Preston.

Before her parents married, Mary's mother, Rachel Rishton, was also a milliner. Rachel's father, Joseph Rishton, ran The Cricket Inn in Albert Street, Preston. A wonderful blog, Pubs in Preston, confirmed that Joseph was in charge of the inn from 1869 to 1891 and during that time he opened a bowling alley. A local newspaper article reported that 40 or so friends helped celebrate the opening which lasted until 11pm with a 'vote of thanks to the host and hostess and the singing of the National Anthem'.

The 1911 census confirms that by this time William was a draper and that Joseph assisted in the business. Another son, Arthur, was an engineer and during the First World War served in the Royal Navy. His final ship was HMS *Dartmouth*. In May 1917 the ship was involved in the Battle of the Otranto Straits in the Adriatic Sea. As the *Dartmouth* returned to port she was hit by a torpedo from a German submarine. Arthur was killed and buried at sea. I found his details on a website – www.AStreetNearYou – where he is listed as an engine room artificer, together with a photograph of him in his uniform. His details are included on the Plymouth Naval Memorial.

Corfe Castle is a ruin perhaps made all the more famous because of it. Although it was built in the 11th century it is known more for its connection with the English Civil War. During this period it was owned by Sir John Bankes – an owner of land throughout Dorset. By 1645 it was one of the last Royalist strongholds and after a siege the castle was left in ruins. John's wife, Mary née Hawtry, was in charge of the castle at this time (John was in London) and she was eventually forced to another family home – Kingston Lacy near Wimborne Minster. As a mark of her courage she was allowed to keep the keys to the castle and they are on display at the National Trust property.

Banff

017244
25 August 1910
Miss Dorothy Fieldgate
7 Junction Road
Gillingham
Kent
England
My Dear Little Dorrie
There is a nice beach here like Ramsgate. Hope you are well.
Dada

Little Dorrie Dorothy Fieldgate was born in 1906 in Maidstone, to parents Harold and Alice née Green. The couple had two other children – Vera and Harold.

In 1901 the family lived in Chatham and Harold was an oyster merchant. By 1911, he had become a canteen manager with the Merchant Navy.

At some point after 1911 the family relocated to Somerset where, in 1914, Harold, who was born in Brightlingsea, Essex, appears in a trade directory for Taunton running a fried fish shop in the High Street.

Later, Vera married Alan Emerson, an inspector of taxes from Frome.

Harold married and became the manager of a grocer, baker and wine merchant's in Wellington.

Dorothy married Edward Lamacraft from Newton Abbott, Devon. In 1911 Edward lived with his family in Dunster, Somerset where his father, Joseph, was a highway surveyor for the district council. Dorothy and Edward eventually lived in Timberscombe, not far from Dunster.

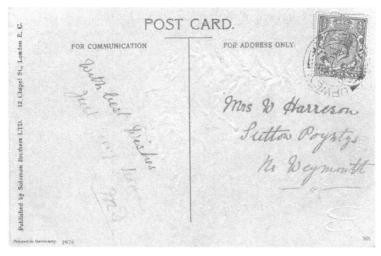

018203
23 December 1913
Mrs W Harrison
Sutton Poyntz
Near Weymouth
With best wishes. Just going home.
MD

Jemima King-Butler and William Harrison married in 1881. William was a carpenter and wheelwright, born in East Coker, Somerset in 1855. The couple had nine children and by 1911 one had died. Those listed as living at the family address in Sutton Poyntz in 1911 were:

William (carpenter), Frederick (wheelwright), Edward (builder), Emily (dressmaker) and Elizabeth (apprentice milliner). Walter and Herbert were at school.

Finding Edward, who was born in 1888, at the home address in 1911 was a surprise. In 1909 he had sailed to New York and appears in the 1910 US census return for Erie in Pennsylvania, living as nephew to Joseph and Annie Smith.

Annie was Jemima's younger sister and she and Joseph had married in Canada in 1892. Joseph was a Dorset man. Their children, Mabel, Henry, Gordon and Dellacourt, were all born in Canada. Sometime after 1904 the family moved to Pennsylvania.

Edward returned to America after 1911 and next appears in American records in 1914 when he married Mary Hammer, who was born in Pennsylvania in 1894. In May 1917 he enlisted in the US army and his occupation is given as pattern-maker, employed by General Electric. At this time the couple had two children. Back in the UK, Herbert enlisted with the RAF in July 1918. Henry Smith claimed exemption from the US army in 1917 on the basis that he had a dependent family – a wife and child. He is listed as an employee with the Nu-Bone Corset Company. The Erie local history Facebook group has a lovely photograph of the company's large and busy office, taken in 1928.

Jemima, who received the postcard, had other family members in Canada. Her brother Joshua married Martha Harrison in 1891 in Ontario, Canada.

Of course, the 1911 census for the Harrison family wouldn't be the first to list all the children, irrespective of them being present at that date. I did consider that perhaps Edward hadn't returned to Dorset in time for the census. However, he appears in a passenger list in April 1911 – 12 days after the census was taken on 2 April – sailing to New York with a final destination of Pennsylvania. His stay in America was not destined to be a long one. He died in 1920 and his death certificate gives the cause as influenza and pneumonia.

Gloucester Cathedral from the Paddock

019217
21 July 1910
Mr Willie Messer
21 Waldeck Street
Whitley
Reading
Dear Willie
I thought you would like this view. I am having a good time got lost in some fields the other night. I say, there is plenty of spooning going on down here. Will write a letter soon. Thank sis for her letter & Mam.
With love to all.
Annie

Willie (William) Messer was born in 1898 – brother to Annie who was born in 1894. Although the children were born in the Reading area, their parents – James and Fanny née Spreadbury – were born in Sixpenny Hanley, Dorset and Houghton, Hampshire.

In 1911, James Messer was a police sergeant. Twenty years earlier he was living with his parents, Joseph and Eliza, in Leckford, Hampshire. Joseph and James are listed as agricultural labourers and the family lived in Keepers Lodge. Based on the listings in the 1891 census, the Messers' home was part of the Leckford Estate – later by bought by John Lewis as his home. It's now managed as part of the Waitrose group.

Annie, who sent the postcard, was a milliner and she married Tom Noakes in 1924. His family were bootmakers. Although Tom is listed as an apprentice in the business, he later appears as a tailor – perhaps that's how he and milliner Annie met.

Willie served in the Royal Navy during the First World War. His service records describe him as having grey eyes and a sallow complexion. Before joining the navy his occupation was science student.

In 1921 Willie married Dorothy Savage and the couple moved away from Berkshire. By 1939 Willie had become a headmaster in Lancashire. When Dorothy died, her probate records give her address as The County Training College in Alsager, Cheshire.

Who was 'sis' mentioned in the postcard? She wasn't a sister – the 1911 census confirms this. Was she a friend? A neighbour? Walking up and down their street via the 1911 census return didn't reveal anyone who might have had the pet name of sis – although that can't be offered as definitive research. In my first book I was able to trace more than one postcard sender by matching their handwriting to the 1911 census – another reason why this document is so useful.

POST CARD.

THIS SPACE CAN BE USED FOR INLAND
CORRESPONDENCE ONLY.

THE ADDRESS ONLY TO BE
WRITTEN HERE.

With love Winnie

THE "NATIONAL" SERIES. (PRINTED IN BRITAIN.)

My dear E.
Thanks for P.C. Sorry I
have not written before.
Glad to hear you
are all keeping well,
we have all had
colds. We have not
heard from J. since
she has been back.

Miss Smith
"The Limes"
Pennington
Nr Lymington

Broomielaw, Glasgow

020221
29 November 1906
Miss Smith
'The Limes'
Pennington
Nr Lymington
My dear E
Thanks for PC. Sorry I have not written before. Glad to hear you are all keeping well, we have all had colds. We have not heard from J since she has been back.
With love Winnie

Evelyn Smith was born in Northaw, Hertfordshire in 1878. No more than two years later her family, father Joseph and mother Emily née Walter, had moved to Lymington, Hampshire where Joseph was a dairyman. It was here that a son, Walter, was born in 1880. In 1891 the family appears in the census at The Chequers Inn where Joseph had become a publican. Now run as a pub and restaurant, its website mentions that it dates back to the 17th century. By the time of the next census, Joseph had reverted to being a dairyman and the family lived at The Limes – a farm, and the address on the postcard.

Joseph was born in Tolpuddle, Dorset in 1851. At the age of only ten he was working as a dairyboy in Holt, a small village near Wimborne Minster, Dorset. His parents, Thomas Smith and Ann née Crocker, had moved from Tolpuddle to a different dairy near Wimborne Minster. It's possible that his parents knew the couple Joseph worked for before this move. Noah and Mary Goodchild were born in Kingston, a small village near Corfe Castle, Dorset. Joseph's parents were born in Bushey, little more than a lane with a few cottages, near Corfe Castle. By 1871, Joseph was back with his parents and siblings in Barton, Hampshire where five members of the large family worked in a dairy. It isn't unreasonable to consider that the dairies around Wimborne Minster and Corfe Castle may have formed part of the Bankes estate – mentioned on page 55.

Although it seems strange that her father became, for a short time, a publican, this might be explained by Evelyn's mother's history. Emily was also born in Northaw and her father had been a licensed victualler.

As well as leaving Dorset for Hampshire and Hertfordshire, Joseph and Evelyn also lived for a while in London – confirmed by the birth of the couple's eldest son, William, in 1877. His entry in the 1911 census, completed by Joseph, gives his son's place of birth as Pimlico.

There's often a belief that in the 19th century families rarely travelled far from their origins. Joseph's parents certainly did, so did the Goodchilds, and Joseph clearly did the same.

The Beach, looking North, Yarmouth

021227
12 August
Miss Clarke
141 Hale End Road
Walthamstow
Essex
D M
Arrived safe at 1 o'clock.
Pleasant journey, weather showery, comfortable lodgings.
Write more later on.
Mother.

This postcard's image is fascinating – ladies wearing elaborate skirts and hats, the men wearing suits and boaters. The time of enjoying the seaside and wearing comfortably casual clothes was still decades away.

May Clarke was born in Walthamstow, Essex in 1880 and she was one of seven children born to Frederick Clarke and Emma née Clover.

Frederick was a gardener. A son, Bert, was also a gardener. Another son, George, served in the First World War and his military records give the address on the postcard and his occupation as printer. Later, in 1939, he is a litho stone printer along with another brother, Sidney.

In 1939, I found a possible May listed as single and a retired shop manageress for a wood store.

Despite Ancestry alerting me to a large number of hints for the family they all turned out to be dead ends. Other family trees included less information than I had discovered. Of course, May's birth certificate would have confirmed if I had the correct May in 1939. Frederick and Emma's marriage records would also have provided more facts to explore a different generation. If you are researching your own family tree and are stumped like I was, buy a certificate to eliminate or confirm details so that you are able to move on with certainty.

Although this particular tree doesn't lead too far, the image of Emma arriving for a break by the seaside is an interesting one. She had grown up in Mendlesham, a small village in Suffolk, and I'm sure she benefited from the fresh air of Norfolk.

Winter Gardens, Yarmouth

022372
19 September 1911
Mrs Ling [sic]
132 Lower Park Road
Peckham, London
192 Northgate Street
Great Yarmouth
Dear N
Still having a ripping time. Weather grand. Arthur has quite made good friends with them hear [sic]. *He goes to bed about half past seven so you see it gives us a few hours to ourselves as the lady here never goes out.*
With Love
M and

George Linge and Ellen née Baker lived in Peckham with their son Edward. George was a police constable from Burnham, Norfolk. In 1891 he is recorded at the police station in Penge. George's father, John, was an innkeeper and the family appears in several records at The Crown in Stanhoe. Their association with the pub began in about 1883 and continued until at least 1916. In 2010 it was renamed The Duck. Before he became an innkeeper John was a coachman and groom. Although George had moved away from Norfolk, his siblings were still mainly in the area and I'm sure he would have enjoyed seeing a card from Great Yarmouth.

It's always useful when a sender of a postcard has added their address, even if it's a temporary one – especially as the family gets a mention in the message.

In 1911, Edith Rudd lived at the address with her four children. The eldest was 11 and the youngest just a few months – so perfect ages for young Arthur to make friends with (although Arthur has not been identified). Edith née Johnson was born in Norwich and she completed the 1911 census. Helpfully, she included the details for her husband's occupation and age (but no name).

Herbert Rudd was born in Diss, Norfolk and was a musician. He served in the army as a drummer and later, in 1911, he appears in Bishop's Stortford as a member of a travelling fair, staying with two other musicians in a boarding house. One of the musicians, Victor Boyce, was born in Great Yarmouth in 1885. His father, William Boyce, was also a musician and played with the Aquarium Orchestra in Great Yarmouth. Musicians accompanied fairs, often performing alongside dancers and singers. The arrival of the fair would be a big event for a community – perhaps the highlight of the year.

It's such a shame not to discover who sent the postcard – but without them adding the address we would not know about Herbert and his musical life.

Goose Fair, Nottingham

023373
Nottingham
22 May 1907
Miss R Watts
48 Market Street
Bridgwater
Somerset
Dear R
Have you enjoyed your holiday.
I am a treat.
We are having lovly [sic] *weather.*
Has Will come home.
Have anyone been for me if so let me know as I thinking of staying until Monday.
Love to all

Walter Watts was born in Carhampton, Somerset in 1852. His father, Thomas, was a blacksmith. From at least 1891 Walter and his wife Amelia née Kitch lived at 48 Market Street where Walter ran his wheelwright business.

Amelia and the couple's six children were all born in Bridgwater. In 1911, sons Edward and William were also wheelwrights in the town. Although at a different address, William was still a wheelwright there in 1939. Another son, Frederick, was a wheelwright in Bristol.

Edward emigrated to Canada around 1913 but returned to Bridgwater to marry Alice Pitman in 1916. The couple lived in Edmonton, Alberta where Edward was a carriage-maker.

Amelia Kitch, Walter's wife, was the daughter of an innkeeper and bricklayer. The family lived at the Cardiff Arms in Bridgwater. This wasn't the first instance I'd come across where an innkeeper had another trade and other innkeepers at the Cardiff Arms also needed a second line of business. In 1891, John Bennett was also a surveyor and ten years later Robert Washer was a tile-maker.

Rhoda, who received the card, remained in the area and died in Bridgwater.

Although the card was sent from Nottingham, the time of year meant that the sender wouldn't have visited the Goose Fair in Market Square (usually held in October).

Market Street in Bridgwater has been developed since the Watts family lived there more than a hundred years ago. When I looked online it was a lovely surprise to see that it's the site of a tyre business – a tenuous link to older times.

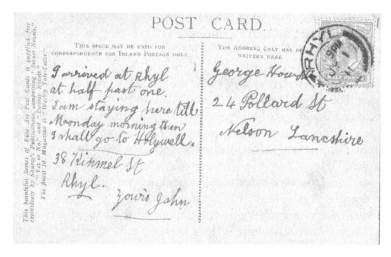

Beheading Stone, Gowan Hill, Stirling

024204
July 1911
George Howorth
24 Pollard Street
Nelson
Lancashire
I arrived at Rhyl at half past one. I am staying here till Monday morning then I shall go to
Holywell.
38 Kinmel Street
Rhyl
Yours John

George and John Howorth were brothers, born in 1885 and 1877, respectively. The 1911 census confirms they lived at Pollard Street with their mother Sarah née Fielding, and another brother, Edmund. The brothers were all cotton operatives. Although Sarah was a widow at this time, she completed the census with the number of years she had been married – 32 – before her husband, James, had died. She also added that she had had eight children and four of them had died. James had been a cotton weaver.

In 1939, John and Edmund lived together as retired cotton operatives. There were more than 20 cotton mills in Nelson. Some of the buildings survive but Pollard Street, where the brothers lived, has been redeveloped and there's little evidence of how it may have looked when the postcard was sent.

A few months before John's visit to Wales, Martha Goffe was landlady at the address in Rhyl. She was a widow, born in Cambridgeshire in 1844. In 1891 she was at Kinmel Street as a lodging house keeper. One of her guests was William Coulson, a journalist and author. He was staying with Mrs Goffe with his wife Ellen and daughter Irene. William was born in Aldershot, Hampshire 1858 and in 1881 he and Ellen lived in London where he was employed as a printer's reader.

Martha's husband, John Goffe, appears with his family at Kinmel Street in 1881. He worked as a railway guard.

Although we don't know why John was visiting Wales, it's interesting to consider his choice of postcard to send home. The message is precise, telling his brother he arrived at half past one, and he also adds his temporary address so that George might write to him there. The view of Stirling has no obvious connection to his trip, but postcards were bought in packs so that people carried a supply and it's possible this card was part of a series he had bought.

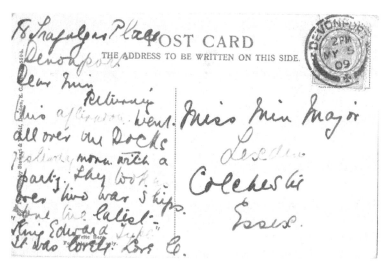

Armada memorial, Plymouth Hoe

025222
5 May 1909
Miss Min Major
Lexden
Colchester
Essex
18 Trafalgar Place
Devonport
Dear Min
Returning this afternoon. Went all over the docks yesterday morn with a party. They took us over two war ships. One the latest 'King Edward Type'.
It was lovely.
Love C

Minna 'Min' Major was born in Lexden, Essex in 1876. In 1911 she lived with her widowed mother, Louisa née Pilgrem, and two sisters, Louisa and Fanny, who were dressmakers. Despite Louisa being a widow, she recorded that she had been married 47 years and had had nine children. She was a corn merchant and this work had continued on from her husband, Horatio Nelson Major, who was born in Great Clacton in 1830. Louisa's parents had died when she was a young girl and she appears in census returns living with her uncle and his wife. Joseph Pilgrem ran the Royal Oak pub in Stoneham Street, Great Coggeshall from at least 1845 until his death in 1875.

Min's father wasn't the only Nelson in the family. A brother born in 1877 was named Nelson Major and another, born in 1874, was named Horatio Nelson Major. He was also a corn merchant. All three appear together in the 1881 census.

Who sent the postcard to Min? It's possible that her sister Clarice had sent it. In 1907 she married Walter Easey, a Methodist minister from Soham, Cambridgeshire. Given the family's own connection with Horatio Nelson, it's fitting that the card was sent from Trafalgar Place.

Out of interest, I wondered how common it was for children to be named after Nelson. A very non-scientific survey based on a search of the 1851 census found there were almost 1700 entries for Horatio and 1000 for Nelson. I continued this train of thought and found that 159 Napoleons were trounced by 180 Wellingtons. Wellington Drummond caught my eye. He was born in 1815 – the year of the battle – at sea. In 1851 he was a clerk with the Bank of England and is listed as Wellington Drummond. He was baptised in Australia as John Duncan Wellington Drummond and was born aboard the convict ship *Marquis of Wellington*. His parents, John and Elizabeth, were free passengers.

Nelson, of Trafalgar fame, died in 1805 – 25 years before Min's father was born. It's a measure of the man's status that at least three members of Min's family were named after him. Construction of the monument in London's Trafalgar Square began in 1840 ensuring new generations would be reminded of him and the battle. My own connection with Nelson is closer to home. Descendants of Lord Nelson lived in Swanage, where I grew up. In fact, the 'Nelson sisters' were neighbours.

I remember visiting their, to me, dark and gloomy house. Propped up against the walls of the hallway were large oil paintings and the elderly sisters only used a couple of rooms on the ground floor. The room that I went into was being used as a bedroom/living room. Geraldine died in 1982 and Mary in 1984. Edward Agar Horatio Nelson, 5th Earl Nelson of Trafalgar and Merton, died in 1951 and is buried in Swanage – as are the sisters.

Special schedules for vessels were introduced in 1851, although none are known to survive from that year, so in practice 1861 was the first year to include returns from the Royal Navy and merchant shipping, at sea and in ports at home and abroad—
The National Archives

Nelson Centenary

026370
September 1905
Miss A Parker
Holywell
Water Side, Wotton-under-Edge
Gloucestershire
One for your collection from A & W F
E. Dulwich
London

Alice Parker (b.1880) was one of three siblings living at the address with their parents, George and Martha, in 1901. George was born in Wotton-under-Edge in 1859. Two of their children, Alice and Arthur, were born in Northamptonshire and Alexander was born in Gloucestershire. Another son, George, was a railway porter and was also born in Northamptonshire, in 1879.

George senior was a gardener and had moved around the country – in 1881 the family were in Berkshire but he is listed as unemployed. Ten years later the family are in Marston St Lawrence, Northamptonshire where George was the head gardener for Burleigh Hall. In 1958 the almost derelict house and grounds were sold and today the land forms part of the campus of Loughborough University.

In 1911, Arthur worked at the family's home address as a photographer and Alexander was a painter and paper hanger. George declared in the census that the couple had had eight children and that four of them had died. Sadly, they were to lose another child the following year. Arthur died in December 1912 from tuberculosis – TB.

Who sent the postcard? Alice's mother, Martha née Francis, was born in Westminster, London in 1853 and the card is from East Dulwich. With Martha's London roots it's clear that perhaps the card was sent from the London branch of the family. Martha's father, Matthew, was a police constable from Essex.

In 1871, Martha is listed as a servant to John Shaw Stewart, a justice of the peace. John was a widower at this time and his young children were with him at the address – including Helenor who would years later marry Frank Gore-Browne, a barrister from New Zealand, and eventually become Lady Gore-Browne. Her sister-in-law, Ethel Gore-Brown, married Hugh Fortescue Locke King who financed Brooklands in Weybridge, Surrey – the first permanent race-track in the world.

Very often I read messages that suggest the recipient collects postcards. When I look for new cards to research – either in shops or online – the sellers sometimes have several addressed to the same person. If I can, I buy two or three just to keep something of the collection together.

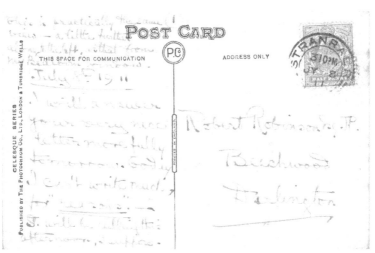

Stranraer: the piers

027320
8 July 1911
Robert Robinson Esq, JP
Beechwood
Darlington
This is practically the same view – a little further along to the left as that from my bedroom window.
I will answer your very nice letter more fully tomorrow.
Today I can't write much for 'reasons'.
J will be calling this afternoon, I suppose.

By 1911, Robert Robinson was a retired civil engineer and widower. With his late wife, Lucy née Pease, he had one daughter – Enid. Lucy was the daughter of a notable Quaker, Thomas Pease, and his first wife, Lucy née Fryer.

The Pease family were originally from Leeds but relocated to the Bristol area where Lucy junior was born in 1844. The family lived at Cote Bank, Westbury-on-Trym – bought by Thomas in 1865 and remaining in the family until the death of Thomas' third wife, Susanna Fry, in 1917. When Thomas died in 1884, his probate records show the place of death as being the Friars Meeting House, Broadmead (a district of Bristol). He is listed in several reports and returns as a gentleman and land owner.

Robert Robinson, who received the postcard, was born in Lancashire in 1838. His father, Thomas, was a farmer. By 1851, Thomas had died and his widow, another Lucy, was the farmer of 400 acres and employer of five labourers. Ten years later, Robert had moved to Durham where he was a civil engineer.

His daughter, Enid, married Dr Charles Steavenson in 1911. The couple lived in Felix House, Middleton St George, Durham where Charles (known as Stanley), is listed as a surgeon. Sometime prior to 1908 Charles contracted TB – 'the biggest killer of its day'. Following the European practices of patients being treated in sanatoriums that benefited from Alpine fresh air, he opened Felix House as a sanatorium. According to an online brochure, he used the Nordrach technique – *the strengthening of the whole organism and so overcoming the disease.*

The house had room for 53 patients – accommodated in 20 chalets similar to those in the Alpine mountains. As well as fresh air and exercise, the patients were treated to goats' milk – avoiding the risk of bovine TB. The doctor kept a large herd which had originated in Switzerland. According to *The Northern Echo*, the Felix Herd was one of the best in this country.

In 1939, the couple were still at Felix House and Enid's probate records confirm she was there until her death.

It's such a shame the writer of the postcard didn't sign it – or reveal more about those 'reasons'. However, the story is not yet complete. In 2010 *The*

Northern Echo ran a story about Enid – one of several, as she and her husband were well-known in the area – and this provides confirmation that it was Enid who wrote the card. A diary written by Enid around 1906 was sold at auction – and an image from the diary confirms the handwriting matches that on the card.

The 1911 census had questions asking about occupation and industry, and a special enquiry into marriage and fertility was carried out at the same time, to shed light on why the birth rate had been falling since the 1870s—The National Archives

New Promenade and Gardens,
Blackpool.

New Promenade and Gardens, Blackpool

028228
20 August 1912
Mr C Birkin
Carlton Street
Cheltenham
Gloucestershire
Dear C
Spending a few days here.
This new promenade is now being constructed.
When finished the whole promenade will be 5 miles long and the two new piers will make five in all.
The weather is fine but no sunshine. There are thousands of people here.
AM

A year before Charles Birkin received this postcard, he lived at a different address in Cheltenham – Denmark Villas – with his wife Mary née Jones. The couple had three children and Charles was a shop assistant.

His parents, James Birkin and Hannah née Townsend, lived at the address on the card – suggesting that perhaps Charles and his family may have moved to Carlton Street after the 1911 census. James' entry in the census describes him as a former gardener who was an invalid due to 'shaking palsy' – possibly what we would recognise today as Parkinson's disease. He died in 1913 and without the benefit of today's medicines and carers, his life and that of his family would have been almost unbearable.

James and Hannah had nine children and two had died by 1911.

Eva became a nurse and in 1939 she was living in Gloucester. Her sister, Florence, became a nursemaid and in 1911 she was living in Leicestershire and working for a vicar and his family. Daniel was a farm labourer and during the First World War he served in the Veterinary Corps.

Mary née Jones – Charles' wife – grew up in Chedworth, Gloucestershire. On the census returns that I traced, Mary's mother is listed as a widow working as either a shopkeeper or grocer.

Blackpool's 'new promenade' was opened by Princess Louise in 1912 – the first year that the illuminations were displayed in the style recognised today. A local history website revealed that by 1910 more than four million visitors were travelling to Blackpool each year and many of them would be catered for by almost 3,500 landladies. I wasn't able to confirm this figure but the properties would range from one or two rooms that were let out, to more formal boarding houses and small hotels.

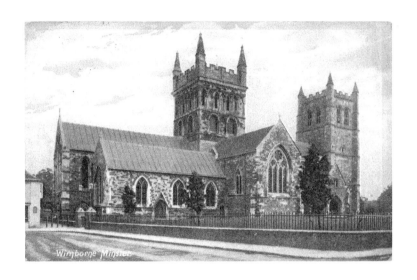

Wimborne Minster

029232
September 1904
Mr AR Creswick
Johnstone's Estate Office
Weymouth
Amy and I are leaving here on Monday, should like to see one of any photos. Hope you and
P arrived home safely. 'Oh dear', my holiday is drawing to a close.
LF

Researching a postcard that was posted to a recipient's place of work can prove difficult. However, Arthur Creswick was relatively easy to locate in the census returns. He was born in Ecclesfield, Yorkshire in 1885. By the time of the 1891 census return the family had moved to Lancashire where Arthur's father – Arthur senior – was a steam engine-maker and turner.

By 1901 the family had moved again – this time to Weymouth, Dorset where Arthur was a torpedo fitter in a factory established in the second half of the 19th century. Robert Whitehead's company was eventually taken over by the British Admiralty at the outbreak of the First World War.

Arthur and Ada née Hulley had four children – two more sons, Percy and Maurice, and a daughter, Mabel Ada Winifred.

By 1911, Arthur – who received the card – had left home and was a boarder in Trowbridge, Wiltshire where he worked as a land agent's clerk for the county council. He next appears in the 1920 US census return as a clerk living with his wife, Joan, in Essex, New Jersey.

Arthur's parents and siblings also appear in American records. In 1940 the widowed Arthur senior is living with Winifred and her husband, William Matthews, a salesman who was born in England.

Percy became a manager with a telephone company and married Elsie, who was born in New Jersey.

Maurice married Clara Ansell in England and they appear in America where he is listed as a tool-maker.

It was a surprise to see all the family (when the children were adults) had emigrated to America. They seemed to have good jobs in this country and lived in an area that to many would be appealing. Perhaps those good jobs held no real sense of financial security?

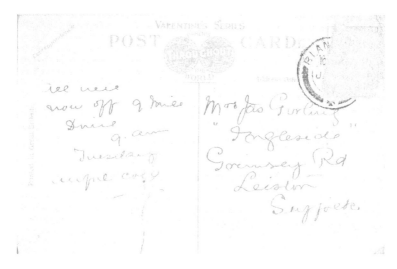

Market Place, Blandford

030235
Mrs James Girling
'Ingleside'
Grimsby Road
Leiston
Suffolk
All well.
Now off 9 miles drive.
9 am Tuesday. Awful cold.

The postcard was sent to Leiston-born couple James Girling and Martha née Woolnough. It's such a shame the sender of the postcard didn't sign their name – and that the stamp has been removed so we can't know when the card was sent from Blandford. In 1911, the couple lived with their two children, schoolboy Percy and Mabel, a teacher. Also at the address was a sister of Martha's, Clara.

Both James and Martha were from large families and it wasn't possible to trace all their siblings beyond their births. However, Jesse Girling appears in emigration records with his wife Julia and their three children. In 1911 the family had left Britain for Ottawa.

In 1881, Martha is recorded as a 15-year-old servant visiting her sister, Rosa, and brother-in-law, Ishmael Girling – James' cousin. Apart from them living in the same road as James and his family, the marriage of her sister undoubtedly confirms that James and Martha knew each other for many years before their own marriage in 1889.

James and several of his brothers were engineers or involved in associated trades. As head of the household in 1911, James recorded that he was a threshing machine erector and worked for agricultural machinery manufacturer Garrett and Sons Ltd who were based in Leiston. They began trading in 1778 when Richard Garrett worked as a blacksmith. The company produced steam engines, steam lorries, trolleybuses and machine tools. In 1806 they built the first horse-powered threshing machine. Although the family eventually withdrew from the company, it continued to trade until the 1980s.

The view on the postcard of Blandford, Dorset hasn't changed much over the years. The area where you see the carriage is now a car park and used for a weekly market. The small building in front of the church is the Pump House, now a water fountain, built in 1760 after the town's devastating fire. Much of the town was rebuilt by two brothers – the Bastards. Many of the 'new' buildings carry commemorative plaques mentioning the Bastard family.

St John's Church, Frome

031237
4 February 1910
Mr F Wallis
33 Church Street
Seaford
Sussex
Dear Frank
Just a card to say I shall be at LB by 5 o'clock if not raining. S with me, hoping to come as far as Fenchurch Street with you and have a little chat on the way.
Bye for now
I remain your Old Chum
Arthur William Cooper

At the beginning of this book I use the words 'Take great care of these people, their lives were as precious to them as yours is to you' as a reminder of the importance of each life, despite the swiftness of revealing their births and deaths within the context of my research. With that in mind I was still surprised at how this card affected me.

Frank Wallis was born in Battersea, London in 1887. In 1911, just weeks before the census return was completed, he married Alice Chester who was born in Hornchurch, Essex in the same year as Frank who was a hairdresser. The next fact that I discovered was that Frank was killed in the First World War. So, within a few searches I had Frank's birth, marriage and death. Of course there was more to find but knowing Frank died in Brook War Hospital, Shooter's Hill, Woolwich in October 1918 was a sobering moment. His widow, Alice, never remarried and died in 1949.

Frank had two brothers – John and William. John served in the Royal Engineers during the First World War with an inland waterways and dock company. In 1911 he had been a lighterman (an operator of a flat-bottomed boat used for loading and unloading ships). After the war he continued with this work, confirmed by the 1939 register.

William was a cycle fitter and in 1911 he lived in The Lodge, Langtons, Hornchurch. His parents, John and Mary née Smith, were also at Langtons at this time, albeit they appear in a different census return. John was a gardener and Mary a housekeeper.

Langtons House is a Grade II 18th century house and in 1929 it was gifted, along with its landscaped gardens, to the local authority by William Varco Williams – John and Mary's employer in 1911. He was the son of Samuel Williams who, according to www.UpminsterHistory.net (an excellent resource), 'had bought 30 acres of land at Dagenham Breach and built a timber dock on the Thames with a railway line connecting with the London Tilbury & Southend railway line. The new Dagenham Dock was mainly used for coastal coal deliveries from the north of England and Samuel Williams' company spent years filling in the marshland and lake behind his dock with soil excavated from the London Underground system transported in Williams' own fleet of lighters'.

The mention of lighters ties in very nicely with John's employment as a lighterman from at least 1911 to 1939 and beyond. He lived in Dagenham throughout that period and, although unproven, is likely to have worked for Samuel Williams and Sons Ltd.

Who sent the postcard? Arthur William Cooper lived in Church Lane, Seaford (just a few yards from Frank's home) and worked as a boot repairer. He was born in Haggerston, London in 1884. Beyond that I wasn't able to follow Arthur's tree – there were too many 'might be' results. Of course, there's no proof this Arthur was Frank's chum – perhaps it's just a coincidence?

The 1921 census should have been taken on 24 April, but was postponed by almost two months in the wake of the Black Friday strike by coal miners, railwaymen and transport workers. This is the only time that the census date has had to be changed—The National Archives

Sidmouth

032250
27 January 1909
Miss M Marchment
c/o Rev HD Lewis
Crewkerne Vicarage
Somerset
ECL
Sidmouth

It can often be frustrating trying to research someone who was, in 1911, an employee. In 1911 Amelia Marchment was working for the Reverend Henry Lewis in Crewkerne as a cook. Fortunately I eventually managed to find Amelia, who was born in Hampshire in 1887. Her parents were Henry Marchment and Jane née Benham. Henry was a farmer and several of Amelia's siblings were farm workers.

Amelia married Cecil Lye in 1915. He was born in Crewkerne and was awarded the Silver War Badge in the First World War – issued to those who were honourably discharged due to injury. In 1939 he is listed as a wine and spirit trade traveller.

Looking at Amelia's employer, I initially struggled to discover more than what was on the 1911 census. A search found a mention of Henry Durbin Lewis and his family in a book – *The Church of Ireland in County Kerry* by JA Murphy. Samuel Lewis, Henry's father, was also a vicar and was born in 1813 in County Sligo. The book carries an excerpt from *Freeman's Journal* of July 1850 that details problems Samuel was experiencing in Dingle. The excerpt begins with a report of two boys being prosecuted for disturbing church services and continues with further incidences:

Divine service was interrupted… it was disturbed by crowds of boys singing and shouting outside the church… there were about 40 persons there at one time, but in the morning 300 persons had pursued me through the streets, some of them singing songs, others whistling… I have been struck with stones three times. I have not knowingly given any provocation; I received threatening notices almost every post threatening my life if I did not leave Dingle.

The book also provided more information about the family. Henry's mother was Sophia Jane Durbin who was born in Gloucestershire in 1820.

Although the 1911 census listed Henry as being married, his wife was not at that address at this time. I eventually found her – Emma Caroline née Corven was born in 1863 in Limerick and the couple married in 1897. The marriage register provided the final piece of the puzzle for this postcard. The initials on the card – ECL – are for Emma Caroline Lewis and this is confirmed by her signature on the marriage register. In 1911 she was a visitor in Westbourne, Bournemouth. The head of the household included the information that she had no children.

Exploring the employer from a census return can often yield some interesting facts – in this case it was the final piece of the jigsaw.

In 1851, two voluntary enquiries were included as part of the census – one into religion and one into education. The report on religion sold over 21,000 copies—The National Archives

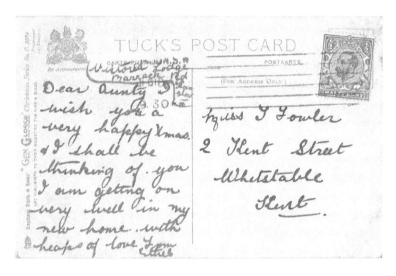

033218
December
Miss T Fowler
2 Kent Street
Whitstable, Kent
Victoria Lodge, Barrack Road
Hounslow
Dear Aunty
I wish you a very happy Xmas and I shall be thinking of you. I am getting on very well in my new home.
With heaps of love from Ethel.

Tammy (b.1861) and her sister, Anna (b.1855), were spinsters, living in Whitstable. Their family was a large one – I traced eight children in all. Their father, William Fowler, was a policeman in Faversham, where the children were born. His career can be traced through the census returns from constable to sergeant. After his retirement he worked as a basket-maker. The children's mother, Ann née Philips, was born in Faversham in 1821.

Tammy and Anna's brothers' jobs included basket-maker, whitesmith (iron and steel finisher, including filing, burnishing or polishing) and brickmaker. George became a carman and later, in 1891, licensed victualler of the Three Tuns in Faversham. The pub is still there today. It was built in 1605 and according to its website, is 'reputed to be the base from which Admiral Lord Nelson recruited and paid his naval crew'. In 1881, another brother, Alfred, appears in the census return at the Hitchin workhouse where he was assistant to the master. His first wife, Mary née Wise, was the workhouse's schoolmistress.

Alfred was at the workhouse from 1877 – when he was an industrial trainer; a role he kept until 1882 when he became master. After the death of Mary he married for the second time. Fanny née Walker appears in the census returns at the workhouse as his wife in 1891 and in 1901 as matron. Before her marriage, Fanny is listed as working for her father who was a butcher.

During his time at the workhouse, Alfred made a scale model of the building and it's held by Hitchin's museum. He left the workhouse in 1903 and became an estate agent. Alfred had children with both wives, including Alfred junior with Fanny. He served in the RAF during the First World War and was killed in September 1918. His name appears on the Arras Flying Services Memorial in France.

The Christmas card was sent by Tammy's niece, Ethel – the daughter of her brother Frederick who died in 1908. Victoria Lodge, where Ethel was working at the time the card was sent, was a home for motherless children. It opened in 1905 and provided a home for 45 children. It closed in 1920.

Stanley Park, Vancouver, British Columbia

034344
Mrs John Scillitoe
Willow Cottage
America Farm
Earls Colne
Essex
England
Will is starting for England on November 3rd from Quebec on Empress of France and I am in Vancouver, 800 further the other way. I will write to you as soon as I have an address.
Minnie

Almost all the postcards I've researched begin with either the 1901 or 1911 census and in 1911 I found the Scillitoe family at the farm and assumed that I was on my way to tracing Minnie and Will.

The family lived at the farm from at least 1891. Jeremiah and Maria Scillitoe had at least six children who either worked on the farm or in the local silk industry.

It soon became clear that Minnie and Will were unlikely to have been siblings of either Jeremiah or Maria.

The card was not sent to Maria Scillitoe, but to Alice née Farthing, the wife of their son John, who ran the farm after Jeremiah retired. Later, in 1939, I found many of John's siblings living in cottages associated with America Farm.

But who were Minnie and Will? I found the answer with Alice Farthing's sister – Edith Minnie Farthing and her husband William Spooner.

I knew from the postcard that Will was returning to England in the November of an unknown year as a passenger on the *Empress of France*. I found him in the passenger lists arriving in Liverpool on 10 November 1920. The couple had married in Essex in 1897. In 1911 they ran a refreshment and commercial house in Braintree.

The couple first appear in Canadian records in 1913 and lived in Edmonton, Alberta. They weren't the only family members to emigrate. Will's sister Cecilia arrived in Canada in 1905. In 1906 she and her husband William Jepp, a carpenter from Essex, lived in Edmonton. William served in the First World War until August 1918 when he suffered a gunshot wound to his right arm.

Both couples appear many times as passengers sailing to and from England, and this is a great example of how often family members returned home for visits. Remember, these people weren't necessarily wealthy. They managed to save enough to keep returning. Today, travelling back is still an expensive and big event; imagine how it must have felt for these folks to return home – and more than once.

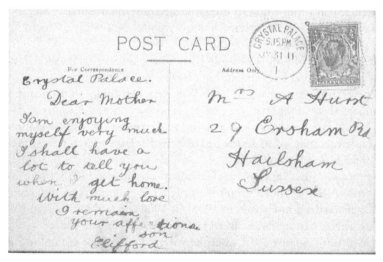

Canada

035345
31 July 1911
Mrs A Hurst
29 Ersham Road
Hailsham, Sussex
Crystal Palace
Dear Mother
I am enjoying myself very much. I shall have a lot to tell you when I get home. With much love, I remain
Your affection son, Clifford

Clifford Hurst was the only child of Horace Hurst and Augusta née Powell and was born in Portslade, Sussex in 1897. His parents had married in 1896 when Horace was 65. His first wife, Frances Linberry, had died in 1890. Their daughter, also Frances, died five years later. Horace was a farmer and Clifford would become an estate agent. In 1939, Clifford and his mother still lived together at the address on the postcard. Augusta's father, Robert Powell, was a grocer and later a house agent in Brighton. Clifford served in the First World War and in 1944 he married Mary Kennett, who was born in Eastbourne.

What might Clifford have to tell his mother? The card has a Crystal Palace cancellation mark and it's likely that he visited the Festival of Empire that was held at Crystal Palace to celebrate the coronation of George V. The festival ran from May to October.

Perhaps the postcard was bought at the festival – emigration to Canada was heavily advertised at this time. When I researched the postcards for the first book in this series, I was surprised at how many families had branches that had emigrated to Canada. During the early years of the 20th century, unemployment was on the increase. The legacy of the Industrial Revolution meant that many communities lived in heavily polluted conditions. The idea of leaving all this behind and providing new labour for the developing regions of Canada must have been attractive to many – millions, in fact.

Clifford's postcard offers four views chosen to appeal to anyone considering emigration. Wide streets, new infrastructure and farming in fresh air would have been appealing sights. John Obed Smith, whose contact details appear on the card, was born in Birmingham in 1864. At the age of 18 he was living and working in Canada where he became a lawyer, most notably in the Manitoba area. In 1908 he came to London in charge of emigration to Canada and remained in that role until 1924.

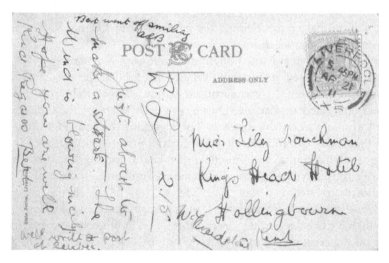

RMS *Empress of Ireland*

036383
21 April 1911
Miss Lily Couchman
King's Head Hotel
Hollingbourne
Kent
D L
Just about to make a start. The wind is blowing nicely.
Hope you are well.
Kind Regards Bert
Will write a post at Quebec
Bert went off smiling
ARB

I'm still surprised at the number of postcards, chosen at random, that lead to stories of emigration. One story from the first book connects with the ship in this postcard – RMS *Empress of Ireland*. Edith Stainer was a maid born in Dorchester, Dorset. She left home to work in Braunton, Devon and then London. Later, she left for Canada. In 1914 she planned to return to England, aboard the *Empress*. During the first night of sailing from Quebec along the St Lawrence River, the ship collided with another. Within fifteen minutes the ship sank and more than 1000 people lost their lives – including Edith. I discovered the story of the *Empress* through a postcard Edith had sent to Dorchester from London. In Canada the tragedy is known as Canada's *Titanic* – more passengers were drowned on the *Empress* than *Titanic* – although the overall loss of life was greater on the *Titanic*.

Back to this postcard. Lillian Couchman lived at the King's Head with her parents, Henry and Emma née Taylor, and brother, Henry. At this time Henry was an articled pupil with an auctioneer and valuer. After serving in the First World War, he became an auctioneer, valuer and estate agent. The Couchman family were at the King's Head for more than 30 years.

Emma, Lillian's mother, had experience of working in a pub before her marriage – in 1881 she worked as a barmaid with her mother Jane née Ward and stepfather William Coppins at the Queen's Arms, Egerton.

Lillian's grandfather, Charles Couchman, was a licensed victualler and farmer at The Roebuck pub in Harrietsham, Kent.

Henry, Lillian's father, had eight siblings and at least two of his nephews emigrated to America and Canada – including Herbert who briefly found himself on my list of possible passengers on the *Empress* as Bert.

Herbert was born in Barnet, Hertfordshire in 1888 and emigrated to Canada where he married Elizabeth Ford in 1909 in Ontario. In the 1921 census he is recorded as Bert.

Another cousin, Walter, emigrated to America in 1871. In 1911 he appears in the Canadian census with his wife Wilena. In 1920 they are back in America where Walter is the proprietor of a hotel in Monroe, New York.

So who might have sent the postcard? I looked for passengers who sailed on the *Empress* on 21 April 1911 with the names of Albert, Bert or Herbert. There were many. Narrowing it down to around Lillian's age and then trying to trace them back to see if I could find a possible connection was unsuccessful. Bert could have been a relative, he could have been a friend. Irrespective of not tracing him, it's clear he meant a lot to Lillian – she had kept his card and also the card that follows this story (bought from the same source but at a different time).

In 1891, for the first time, women census takers were employed. The requirements for a good census taker have not changed much in over 150 years: '...he must not be infirm; he must be temperate, orderly and respectable, and such a person has to conduct himself with strict propriety...'—The National Archives

Cunard Line

037385
25 April 1913
Miss LM Couchman
Kings Head Inn
Hollingbourne
Near Maidstone
Kent
Just got on the boat. Are just going to make a start. Have seen some sights. Tremendous lot of people some crying some laughing.
Write later
R Croucher

Fortunately for me, the second postcard sent to Lillian was signed with a surname and I soon found Rhoda Croucher living in Hollingbourne with her sister, Edith, and widowed father, Charles – their mother, Tamson née Piles, had died in 1896. With those details I was able to trace the family to RMS *Ausonia* in April 1913.

The girls' brother, Charles junior, had emigrated to Canada in 1908 and eventually married Henrietta Alderson, who was born in Toronto, Ontario.

From Rhoda's message on the postcard it's clear that those leaving for Canada had mixed emotions. Would their hopes for a new and better life be fulfilled?

Charles and Henrietta died in 1927 – just a few months apart. Charles senior died in 1931, aged 64.

Edith married George Warden in 1914. He was from Ipswich and had arrived in Canada as a young boy. Rhoda married Frederick Hughes in 1915. Frederick was also born in England and had emigrated in 1913. The sisters and their families settled in Niagara Falls.

Lillian remained in England.

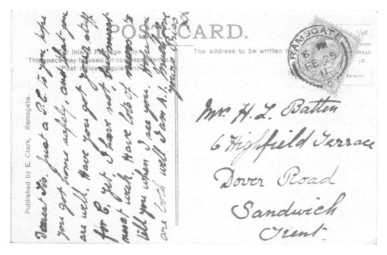

Ramsgate

038225
25 February 1911
Mrs HL Batten
6 Highfield Terrace
Dover Road
Sandwich
Kent
Dearest Sis.
Just a PC to you. Hope you got home safely and that you are well. Have you got your stuff for C yet. I have not but must next week. Have lots of news to tell you when I see you. Hope you are both well. I am AI.
Much love
Yours Priss

Henry Batten and Lily née King were married in 1900. Henry was a gardener. Lily was one of at least nine children born to Alfred and Martha King. Alfred is listed as a farm bailiff who was born in Yalding, Kent. Martha was born in Linton, Kent.

The card is signed by Priss – Lily's sister Priscilla who is listed as Prissie in some census returns. In 1911 she was a nurse working for a baker and confectioner's family in Ramsgate. In 1918 she married Horace Pacy, the son of a hoop-maker, who was born in Staplehurst. In 1939 he is listed as a harness-maker and his short service attestation records from the First World War show he had been an instrument-maker.

Who was C, mentioned in the card's message? Charles King was born in March 1880 and as the card was sent in February, I wonder if perhaps Priss was referring to a birthday present for him, their brother. Charles married Grace Burch, the daughter of a fishmonger, in 1905 in London – where Charles worked as a railway plate layer.

With Priss and Lily having so many siblings I decided to follow just one more – brother Alfred, a farm labourer, who married Lucy Stacey in 1899. By 1911 the couple had seven children and more were born after the census. The eldest daughter I found was Dorothy.

In 1920 she emigrated to Canada and her emigration records show that she was a waitress and was going to work for the Canadian government. Her journey had been funded by the British government. A year later she married Silas Preston from Lancashire. Their marriage records show that he was a machinist and by this time Lucy was an operator.

Most of the families I have researched who had connections with either America or Canada, left the UK before the First World War. It's clear that after the war, the idea of living abroad was tempting enough for a young woman to leave her family and make a new life in Canada.

The Brompton Oratory

039258
25 April 1911
Miss Strange
Caunton Manor, Newark, Nottinghamshire
Tuesday
Dear S
Many thanks for flowers. They are lovely and look so fresh. I hope you are feeling better. Sorry Charlie is laid up. I am going to Southall tomorrow and Bab is coming. She came home yesterday, I will write you after tomorrow. Sorry you are not coming back tomorrow. Much love
Evelyn

Evelina and Laura Strange were the daughters of John Strange and Eliza née Watts and were born in Chippenham, Wiltshire in 1878 and 1885, respectively. John was a coachman from Blunsdon, Wiltshire. Both daughters were employed as servants and their mother, Eliza, appears in the 1861 census as a 13-year-old pupil in a school for female servants in Bath, near her place of birth. She wasn't the youngest pupil – Lucy England and Betsey Hawker were both only 11. John Strange died aged 38 in 1892 and Eliza later married Alfred Carey who was almost 25 years her senior. He was employed as a cemetery caretaker in Chippenham.

Evelina and Laura had the good fortune of working for relatively interesting employers – well, fortunately for me. The postcard Evelina sent was posted in Paddington, London and in 1911 she worked in Paddington for Dr Alfred Mellor, the grandson of John Mellor – a judge and former MP for Great Yarmouth and Nottingham. His son, Alfred's father, was a barrister and polo player.

Alfred Mellor and his wife Dora née Webster had three daughters and would later move to Chippenham – where Evelina and her family lived. Bab, mentioned in the message, could be Barbara Mellor, their youngest daughter – although at the time of the postcard she was only three years old.

In 1911, Laura worked for Samuel Hole at the address on the postcard. Samuel was born in 1862 and is recorded as a major and in some documents as a barrister. He was the son of the Very Reverend Dr Samuel Reynolds Hole DD (doctor of divinity). Samuel senior became Dean of Rochester cathedral where he is remembered by the 'number three bell' that carries this detail: 'In remembrance of S. Reynolds Hole, Dean. Died 27th August – 1904'.

Samuel senior was a noted horticulturist, especially with roses and was the inaugural recipient of the Royal Horticultural Society's Victoria Medal of Honour.

It's rather nice that Evelina is thanking her sister for flowers – although we have no idea if they had any connection with her employer's family's skills.

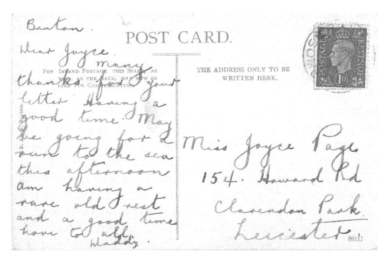

Stourton Church

040277
Miss Joyce Page
154 Howard Road
Clarendon Park
Leicester
Bruton
Dear Joyce
Many thanks for your letter. Having a good time. May be going for a run to the sea this afternoon. Am having a rare old rest and a good time.
Love to all.
Maddy

This view of Stourton Church (near the Stourhead Estate in Wiltshire) is close to home and as I've enjoyed visiting the church I decided to research it, even though it was sent later than most of the cards in this book.

Joyce Page is at the address when the 1939 register was taken and this provided her date of birth – December 1923 – and that of her parents, Frederick (b.1893) and Frances née Jarvis (b.1897). Frederick was a pharmacist/retail chemist and Frances was the daughter of a grocer. The register had been updated to include Joyce's married name – which I will come to later.

Frederick was the son of David Page and his second wife, Emma née Evans. Together, the couple had four children. David was the secretary to a friendly society and before that was a rates collector. David had at least two sons with his first wife, Eleanor née Cowell – Lewis and Vernon. In 1939, Lewis was the headmaster of an elementary school in Leicestershire. Vernon lived for a time in Canada – records from the First World War confirm he was there in 1914 and returned after the war in 1919. He was back in the UK for the 1939 register where he is listed as being a secretary to a friendly society.

Wallace, a full brother to Joyce, also became a teacher and in the 1939 register is listed as headmaster at Sexey's School in Bruton, Somerset. In fact, he was headmaster there from 1927 to 1955. One notable pupil from this period is broadcaster, author and theatre director Ned Sherrin.

Who sent Joyce the postcard? It is likely to have been a sibling. Searches of births after her parents' marriage in 1921 revealed several candidates. However, it wasn't possible to confirm if they were siblings – and none of the first names seemed to fit with what might have been a pet name on the postcard.

Bruton is a relatively short distance from Stourton – and similarly not far from the coast.

"The Hawthorns"
Beaufort Rd
Friday   St Leonard's
                    Sussex

Dear Jack We were very
thankful to get y c [?] to
to say you were landed
in England again.
We can decipher
your left-handed remark
& shall be glad of a bit
more telling us nature
of your wound. I will
write again when I am
sure you will receive it
as I thought perhaps you
were only at a "Clearing
Station". We all send love.
The girls are going back
to Dover tomorrow. We
are all well & hope you
are not having much
pain.   Your aff. mother [?]

POST CARD
THE ADDRESS TO BE WRITTEN ON THIS SIDE.

HASTINGS
9 PM
30 AUG
1918

Pte J. Pollin
24208
W. E. Rents [?]
Ward 38,
Red X Hospital
Netley Southampton

114

041304
30 August 1918
Pte. J Pollin
24208
East Kents
Ward 38
Red X Hospital
Netley, Southampton
'The Hawthorns'
Beaufort Rd
St Leonards, Sussex
Friday
Dear Jack
We were very thankful to get PC and to say you were landed in England again.
We can decipher your left-handed scrawl and shall be glad of a bit more telling us the nature of your wound. I will write again when I am sure you will receive it as I thought perhaps you were only at a 'Clearing Station'. We all send love.
The girls are going back to Dover tomorrow. We are all well and hope you are not having much pain.
Your affectionate mother

Jack's mother, who sent the postcard, wasn't at the address written on the card in 1911. However, because I had Jack's service number, I was able to trace the family.

John 'Jack' Pollin was born in Spalding, Lincolnshire in 1898. His father, William Pollin, was a clothier from Moulin in Lincolnshire. The 1911 census included Jack's mother, Frances née Whittaker, and two siblings: William and Mabel. At this time the family lived in Spalding.

By 1915, William and Frances lived near Dover and in 1939 they were with Mabel in Hastings where William had become a market gardener.

Although Jack's mother must have been terribly distressed that he had sustained an injury, there must have been immense relief that he had returned to England, albeit to a hospital. Jack survived the war and in 1924 married Mildred French. In 1939 the couple were living in Hastings and Jack is listed as a billiard chalk manufacturer.

There is added poignancy to Frances' postcard – just a few months earlier in April 1918, Jack's brother, William, had been killed. His army records reveal that before the war he was a motor cycle belt-maker in Dover. He is listed on the Tyne Cot Memorial in Belgium. The cemetery is the largest for Commonwealth losses in the world.

London Bridge

042319
13 August 1910
Mr E Packer
49 Ponting Street
Swindon
Dear Ernie
We shall be leaving London at 2.28pm.
If you and L could meet us we should like to see you.
Arthur

It's wonderful to consider how precise the train times were more than a hundred years ago – although we can't know if the train actually left on time.

Ernest Packer lived at 41 Ponting Street in 1911. I couldn't find another family with that name in the street and even the listing for Ernest has been amended. Arthur mentions 'L' and it is likely this could be Ernest's wife, Mary Lois née Mann. Ernest was born in Ashton Keynes, Wiltshire in 1874 and was a coach finisher working for the Great Western Railway.

Mary Lois was born in St Buryan, Cornwall in 1881. Her father, William, was a seedsman agent and her stepmother, Millicent née Pearce, was a lodging housekeeper in Morrab Road, Penzance. Later, some of Mary's siblings would run a similar establishment in the same road. Mary Lois' mother, Elizabeth née Mildren, had died in 1882.

Mary Lois had at least nine full and half siblings including brothers Wilfred and William. Wilfred became a dental mechanic, later a dentist. William also entered the dental profession and is listed in 1911 as a dentist's apprentice.

Who was Arthur? I couldn't trace an Arthur within the family's tree. Was he a neighbour or someone who lived nearby? Searching for any Arthurs in the village didn't lead me to match the handwriting on the card.

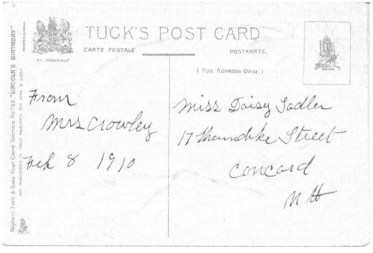

Lincoln's Home, Springfield, Illinois

Miss Daisy Sadler
17 Thorndyke Street
Concord
New Hampshire
From Mrs Crowley
Feb 8 1910

In 1910, Daisy Sadler lived with her aunt and uncle, siblings Horace and Maria Holmes. Also at the address was her cousin, Jesse Chase – the son of another sibling, Alice née Holmes, and her husband, Alfred Chase. Unusually, Jesse also appears in the census return with his parents and brother, Clarence.

Daisy was born in 1880 and was a seamstress in a department store and perhaps this is why she lived with her aunt who was a tailoress. Uncle Horace was a blacksmith. Daisy's parents were James Sadler and Sylvia née Holmes.

Daisy's grandfather, Francis Holmes (b.1816), was a private in the Sharpshooters regiment in New Hampshire and enlisted in 1861. Mustered-out with an injury, he would become a grain dealer.

Francis' son Bradford (b.1845) – Daisy's uncle – also served in the Civil War and was killed on 18 July 1863 at Fort Wagner – aged only 17. Although the minimum age for enlisting was 18 it wasn't uncommon for this to be ignored by recruiting officers. More than 100,000 soldiers in the Union army were not yet 15. Drummer boys as young as nine were accepted.

Private Bradford Holmes was buried in a mass grave in Charleston, South Carolina. Colonel Robert Gould Shaw was killed on the same day (he was aged 25) and buried at the same location. After the war their remains were reburied at the Beaufort National Cemetery in South Carolina.

Although the number of soldiers killed on 18 July could never be accurately confirmed, a report by Confederate General Hagood recorded that he 'buried 800 bodies in mass graves in front of Wagner'.

Robert Gould Shaw was born in Boston in 1837 to an abolitionist family and he accepted command of the first all-black regiment (the 54th Massachusetts). A website mentions that he had 'encouraged the men to refuse their pay until it was equal to that of white troops' wage'. The profile continues: 'Shaw was killed while leading his men to the parapet of the Confederate-held Fort Wagner. Although the regiment was overwhelmed by firing from the defenses and driven back, suffering many casualties, Shaw's leadership and the regiment became legendary. They inspired hundreds of thousands more African Americans to enlist for the Union helping to turn the tide of the war to its ultimate victory'.

The story of Shaw and the regiment was dramatised in the 1989 film *Glory*. Although this is by no means a documentary, the film begins with a statement that Shaw 'wrote home regularly... These letters are collected in the

Houghton Library of Harvard University'. Throughout the film, Shaw's letters provide an insight, albeit dramatised, into the lead-up to the battle and aftermath.

Like many American families, the lineage of the Holmes ancestry is officially documented through their connections with the Civil War and or the American Revolution. The Holmes family is recorded in The Daughters of the American Revolution directory as descended from Mather Holmes (b.1756) and Philip Holmes (b.1731), Francis' grandfather and great-grandfather, respectively. The family's entry states:

Mather Holmes served several enlistments under Captains Penniman and Endicott. Philip Holmes enlisted in Captain Peter Talbot's company at the Lexington Alarm.

The Battle of Lexington and Concord began in Lexington in April 1775. Several hundred men had gathered in the town to defend their stash of ammunition from the advancing British redcoats. These local men were a civilian population of mainly farmers, blacksmiths and shopkeepers.

The Daughters was founded in 1890 and today there are estimated to be 185,000 members who 'form lifelong bonds, honor their revolutionary ancestors and promote historic preservation, education and patriotism in their communities'.

United States federal census dates

1820 – 7 August

1830 – 1 June

1840 – 1 June

1850 – 1 June

1860 – 1 June

1870 – 1 June

1880 – 1 June

1890 – 2 June

1900 – 1 June

1910 – 15 April

1920 – 1 January

1930 – 1 April

1940 – 1 April

Erie, Pa. 12/21/06
Merry X-Mas, and a Happy
New Year. Just saw
Myron Talmadge a minute
ago. Said he would
wish you Merry
X-Mas for
me.
Return
the
comp.
for me.
Rea

"LONG
MAY
SHE
WAVE."

POST CARD
NAME AND ADDRESS ONLY ON THIS SIDE

Prof. H. A. Weyland,
242 Glenburn
Brooklyn
N.Y.
Hamilton Art School

Hamilton
Ont,
Canada

044364
Professor HA Neyland
Hamilton, Ontario, Canada
Brooklyn, New York
Erie, Pennsylvania
21 December 1906
Merry Xmas and a Happy New Year. Just saw Myron Talmadge a minute ago. Said he would wish you Merry Xmas for me. Return the comp for me.
Rea
Hamilton Art School

Given the mention of Hamilton Art School it's not surprising to discover that Harry Neyland was an artist. One website describes him as a painter, sculptor and illustrator. He studied at the Zanerian Art College in Columbus, Ohio, Pratt Institute in Brooklyn and the Art Students' League in New York City.

After completing his studies, Harry became the first art director of the New York Military Academy in Cornwall-on-Hudson. He taught at the Hamilton Art School in Ontario until 1908 – which ties in nicely with the postcard being sent in 1906. In 1911, he settled in New Bedford, Massachusetts where he served as director of the Swain Free School of Design until 1930.

Looking at his work online it's clear that he 'was fascinated by old sailing vessels'. He spent time in England and France, studying at the Académie Julian and the Académie Colarossi in Paris – confirmed by his appearance in a number of passenger lists.

Harry was born in Erie, Pennsylvania in 1877. His father, George Neyland, was one of at least 13 children. George's parents, Daniel and Mary née McMahon, had emigrated to America from Ireland in around 1842. Their children were either born in Ireland or, like George, in America.

George's brother Patrick was the first son that I traced and he was born in Ireland in 1837. Like at least one other brother, he served in the Civil War. Another brother, Daniel, moved to Liberty Lake, Washington. With his wife Louisa he founded a store near Lake Loomis. An article published in *The Splash* (Liberty Lake's community paper) in 2011 describes the store:

It would have been typical of a country store of that era and most likely sold everything a farming family needed. At a country store, one could find groceries and staples, hardware, medical supplies, laundry goods, sewing provisions, toys, tobacco and candy. It also was a place for socializing, and one might have enjoyed a game of checkers. Yet it would have been unique in that it rented boats and stocked more items for fishing and other lake activities.

By 1907 the Neyland family developed the business and had established a resort with 20 cabins – named Neyland's Grove. The family ran the business until the 1940s.

Harry, who received the postcard, died in 1958. You can find some great examples of his work online, including illustrations for books about sailing and sailors.

The 1921 census was the first to provide for separate confidential returns to be made by individuals within a household if they so wished. The 1911 enquiry into fertility was dropped—The National Archives

Grant's Tomb, Riverside Drive, New York

045343
Mr Phil Goatcher
Rochester Lodge
Collins Place
Melbourne
Australia
New York /9/4/10
Kind Regards
John G Carr

Phil Goatcher appears in Australia as a scenic artist in an electoral register of 1912. Other searches revealed a fascinating story that begins with his birth in St Pancras, London in 1851. Philip William Goatcher was one of at least six children born to Philip Goatcher and Mary née Betts. Philip senior was a man of many trades and he is listed in census returns and registers as a policeman, inspector of nuisances [sanitary inspector] gas inspector, licensed victualler and other jobs associated with those roles. In 1891 he and Mary lived in Asylum Road, Peckham and it's likely that they may have run the Asylum Tavern, as it is known today.

Philip junior (known as Phil) was well travelled and he appears in passenger lists sailing to America and Australia. In 1875 he married his first wife, Alice Little (the daughter of a cab proprietor), in Paddington, London. In 1880 she appears in the census return for New Jersey with three children – Philip, Louisa and James. In 1910 she is running a boarding house in Westchester, New York. Another son, Arthur, is also at the address.

In 1899 he married his second wife, Emma Stone, in Paddington, New South Wales. It seems such a strange coincidence to marry on the other side of the world in a place named after the location of his first marriage. Emma was almost 25 years Phil's junior. She was born in Australia and her father was a hairdresser. Phil and Emma would have at least two children.

There are many websites that mention Phil Goatcher with images of his work. Knowing that he was a scenic artist led me to some of the most famous theatres in the United Kingdom and abroad. The Goatcher Curtain is a feature in Boulder, Australia's town hall – a former theatre. It has hung in the building since 1908 and tours of the building include the lowering of the curtain by its original pulley mechanism.

Before working in Australia, Phil was principle designer at Wallack's Theatre in New York. In London, he worked in Drury Lane and Covent Garden. He was also associated with Richard D'Oyly Carte at the Savoy Theatre.

He died in Australia in 1931. Emma had died in 1913. Phil's first wife continued to live in America with their children.

Blackstone Hospital, Pawtucket, Rhode Island

046341
Miss May B Lee
58 Moring Road
Upper Tooting, London
Blackstone Hospital
Pawtucket, Rhode Island
Dear Sister
This is our hospital. I often think of you and hope that you are realizing your ambition that of being one of the best painters in the world.
If you do not find it convenient to send letters, send me a postcard once in a while.
Goodbye, with love from your sister.
Daisy.

May Bridges Lee was born in Lahore, India in 1884. She was the daughter of barrister John Bridges Lee and Mary née Merk. John was the son of a chemist in Great Yarmouth, where he was born – along with at least six siblings. John senior was born in Bethnal Green, London in 1820. In 1851, he and his wife Emma appear in a census return for Great Yarmouth where he is listed as a chemist and druggist. After retiring, he and Emma returned to London and they are listed in 1891 as living in Paddington.

John junior – May's father – spent much of his working life in India where he married Mary Merk, the daughter of a vicar. John's brother, Harry, also lived and worked in India and married Alice Obbard there in 1889.

After the death of Mary in 1891, John, May and another daughter, Daisy – who sent the card – returned to England. Daisy would become a nurse and appears in records as leaving England for Canada and then settling in America.

In 1936, May married architect Sir Philip Stott. He was born in Lancashire and as well as being an architect he was also a civil engineer. Sir Philip is best known for designing cotton mills and his first mill, Chadderton, survives and is a listed building. He designed almost 80 mills in the UK and several in Europe and India.

But what of May's aspirations to become one of the best painters in the world? Many of her portraits were of civic dignitaries and hang in town halls around the country. Her portrait of Sir Henry Tyler hangs in the Royal London Hospital for Integrated Medicine, successor to the London Homeopathic Hospital in Great Ormond Street, London. You can see the homeopathic hospital in the next postcard.

Little information is available about Daisy, who sent the card. The message suggests that she and May had lost touch. Daisy became a naturalised American citizen and her application states that she had emigrated from England in 1914.

Children's Hospital & Homeopathic Hospital
Great Ormond Street

047297
17 July 1906
Hugh Miller, Esq
21 Hill Place
Edinburgh
Thought this would interest you, see where I am. You will see name of hospital written above the doorway in the picture on this PC and I have put a dot on it.
Have just come in from a delightful walk and am about to go on duty.
With 'etc'
J

With such clear handwriting it should have been easy to trace Hugh. I had a hunch that he was perhaps a doctor and might have trained with J. A search in Edinburgh led me to Hugh C. Miller (b.1877) who was, in 1901, house physician in Lauriston Royal Infirmary, Edinburgh.

In many records Hugh's name is given as Miller but his registered name is Hugh Crichton-Miller and he was born in Genoa, Italy where his father, Donald, was a Presbyterian minister. Hugh was sent to Scotland to study (his father was born in Fife in 1838). Later, he studied medicine at Edinburgh University, where he wrote his thesis on hypnotism.

Following service in the First World War, where he witnessed the effects of shell shock, he founded a charitable clinic in Tavistock Square, London to treat nervous complaints – a few minutes' walk from Great Ormond Street. He was a friend and contemporary of Carl Jung and would become vice-president of the CG Jung Institute in Zurich.

But is this distinguished Hugh the recipient of the card? In 1903, Hugh Crichton-Miller married Eleanor Lorimer in Edinburgh and in 1906, the year the card was sent, the couple celebrated the birth of their first son, Donald, in Italy.

Whoever the real Hugh is, the card he received was kept, allowing an opportunity to see Great Ormond Street as it was more than a hundred years ago. Today, the street has incorporated a modern entrance to what is now known as Great Ormond Street Hospital for Children, set back so that the main view is still recognisable as the one depicted in the postcard. J's dot is above the hospital's name on the postcard

I'm indebted to the Archive Service, Great Ormond Street Hospital for Children NHS Foundation Trust for suggesting that J might be Dr James Graham Forbes – based on a sample of the Dr Forbes' handwriting in the hospital's archives.

I was told that Dr Forbes later became a noted infectious diseases specialist and I was directed to a website for the Royal College of Surgeons for his biography where it was recorded that he was born in Clevedon, Somerset.

I found Dr Forbes in the 1911 census – which would be completed in his own handwriting. Was that a match to that on the postcard? Well, the 'J' was similar but despite trying hard to convince myself it was him, there was no clear similarity and there was another query – the doctor had stated that he was born in Steeple Claydon, Buckinghamshire. His employment details in 1911 matched those recorded on the RCS website.

It's such a shame not to identify conclusively who sent or received the postcard – it would certainly be wonderful to know who J was. Perhaps she was a nurse – they might even have cared for one or both of the children whose stories follow this one.

In 1908, two years after the postcard was sent, the now demolished Astor Out-patient Wing was opened. This is shown on the far right of the image, under construction. The wing was funded by newspaper magnate William Waldorf Astor, who donated $250,000 in 1903.

The child first and always—Great Ormond Street Hospital

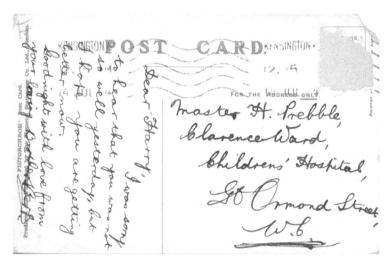

Barnstaple, Pilton

048328
Master H Prebble
Clarence Ward
Children's Hospital
Great Ormond Street
Dear Harry
I was sorry to hear that you was not so well yesterday, but I hope you are getting better now.
Goodnight with love from your loving Brother Bert.

Henry 'Harry' Prebble was only six years old when he was admitted to Great Ormond Street Hospital (a hospital specialising in the care of sick children) in August 1913. The youngest of three children, Harry was born in London and baptised in St Matthew's Church, Kensington. In 1911, the family lived in Earl's Terrace, London – the address given when Harry was admitted to the hospital.

Harry's father, Thomas Prebble, was a constable with the Metropolitan police and was born in Lydd, Kent – part of Romney Marsh. In 1881 he and his family lived in Gut Bank House in Lydd where his father was a fisherman.

He married Ann Gibbons in 1897, the daughter of Robert Gibbons, a broom-maker. Her family lived in Mile End, London.

In 1920, Thomas retired and was granted a police pension of £153 per annum, beginning in the November of that year.

Robert junior – Bert, who sent the card – was born in 1897. He served in the First World War in the Royal Navy and married Lilian Soper in Aylesbury, Buckinghamshire in 1927. In 1939 he was an estimating surveyor and ARP warden, living with Lilian in Ealing.

Harry's sister, Ivy, became a dressmaker.

Harry was admitted to the Clarence Ward in the hospital – named after the eldest son of the Prince and Princess of Wales (the future Edward VII and Queen Alexandra). Albert Victor, Duke of Clarence and Avondale died of Russian flu in 1892. Harry's admission records show he was suffering from nephritis, a disease of the urinary system that affects the kidneys. He died a few weeks later.

Whoe'er thou art, whom
chance may bring
To this sequester'd spot,
If then the plaintive syren sing,

Oh, softly tread beneath
her bower,
And think of heaven's dispo-
sing power
Of man's uncertain lot.

POST CARD.

This space may be used for communication.

The ADDRESS only to be written here,

Serie 2115.

Dear Doris
I received the
card with ma-
ny thanks and
was pleased to
know you are
getting on
from Ada Kildare

Miss D May
Louise Ward
Great Ormond
St
Hospital
London
W C

049329
Miss D May
Louise Ward
Great Ormond Street Hospital
London
Dear Doris
I received the card with many thanks
and are pleased to know you are getting on.
From
Ada Wildman

Doris May was eight years old when she was admitted to the Louise Ward (named after Princess Louise Caroline Alberta who was born in 1848) in 1910. She was treated for an internal abscess and was discharged after 16 days. At this time, home was London Road, Romford, Essex.

Her parents, Jesse May and Jeanie née Siggers, had three children. Jesse was a porter for a drapers' wholesaler and was born in Blean, Kent. Jeanie was born in Whitechapel, London and in 1881 she lived with her family in Nag's Head Yard.

Jesse served in the RAF during the First World War. His service records show that he enlisted with the Royal Navy in 1917 – shortly before the RAF was formed the following year from the Royal Flying Corps.

In 1939, Doris is recorded as working as a secretary for an estate agent and living with her parents and brother, Harold, in Romford. Harold was a clerk with an ironmongery business.

The Historic Hospital Admission Records Project is an excellent resource for anyone researching ancestors who might have been admitted to a children's hospital in London. The searchable database provided me with the additional information about Doris – and Harry, whose story preceded this one.

In Doris' case, the database revealed that she had been admitted to the hospital by Dr Addison. Searching through the 1911 census I found more than one candidate but was able, through other records, to confirm the doctor involved with Doris' case.

Oswald Addison (b.1874) was the son of a solicitor. In 1909 he married Kate Brown (the daughter of a solicitor) and in 1911 the couple lived with her mother, Ada. Oswald is listed in 1911 as a surgeon and Kate (b.1873) is a medical practitioner and specialised in dermatology. In 1910, a medical directory lists the couple's respective specialisms and roles and Oswald's include the hospital for sick children in Great Ormond Street where he was resident medical superintendent. He was also closely associated with several other hospitals, including the Princess Louise Kensington Hospital for Children (named after the same princess as Doris' ward). A business directory from 1930 lists the couple in Harley Street.

The Royal College of Surgeons' website has a full biography of Oswald and mentions that he was a 'painstaking and careful operator, gifted with dexterity and gentleness'. Kate gets a mention within his entry and confirms she was clinical assistant in the skin departments at several hospitals including University College Hospital.

In 1939, Oswald is listed as a retired surgeon and Kate as a retired medical woman. The couple died within a few months of each other in 1942.

It's always interesting to research the sender of a postcard. Doris was admitted to the hospital at an age when she would be very aware of her time away from home and the obvious effects of her illness. Despite those likely traumatic memories, she chose to keep the postcard her friend sent her.

Searching for Ada Wildman in Romford led me to another address in London Road. Ada was born in 1900 in Tottenham. Her father, John Wildman, was a gardener. In 1911, Ada's mother – also Ada – wasn't at the family's address. She is found in Eastwick, Hertfordshire with her parents – attending to her invalid mother, Emma. Emma was born in 1848 and with husband John Springham had 16 children (six had died by 1911).

Ada, who sent Doris the postcard, was hard to trace beyond 1911. Her brother, John, was born in 1906 and he appears in various records as a gardener. Ada is included in one or two online trees, but with only her death in 1982 adding to what I had discovered. However, we do know that she and Doris exchanged cards and were friends – seeing her handwriting and reading her message has opened the door to the good treatment Doris received in hospital.

The Mayflower Connection

In remembrance of your kind
hospitality

May 25 05

A. C. Bosselman, Publisher, New York

050387

Introduction

The 400th anniversary of the *Mayflower*'s sailing from England to the New World in 1620 was celebrated on both sides of the Atlantic. The *Mayflower* wasn't the first ship to take settlers across the Atlantic, but for a number of reasons – not least the celebration of their first Thanksgiving in 1621 – it is the *Mayflower* and her passengers that most of us recognise.

The postcards in this section were all sent during the early years of the 20th century and it is the people associated with those cards who allow us to explore the *Mayflower*'s journey – what happened to those first settlers and the generation that followed. For us, that journey will begin in Dorking, Surrey with the family of William Mullins.

More than 130 passengers and crew sailed aboard the *Mayflower*. Not all the passengers were leaving England in search of religious freedom. For some it was the attraction of new business opportunities. William Mullins was a shoemaker and for him the voyage was very much a commercial deal – he was part of the consortium who funded the crossing. Mullins' business was in West Street, Dorking and the premises are still there today as Mullins Coffee Shop. Their website has some wonderful photographs of descendants of the Mullins family visiting their ancestral roots.

Mullins left home with his wife Alice and two of their children, Priscilla and Joseph, in July 1620. Some records suggest that Alice was William's second wife and the stepmother of one or both of the children. William is known to have older children who remained in England. The family boarded the *Mayflower* in Rotherhithe where it sailed to Southampton.

Although the family survived the crossing, William, Alice and Joseph did not live beyond the first year in America – it's estimated that almost half the passengers died either during the crossing or within that first year.

The Mayflower Connection will mainly follow Priscilla's story.

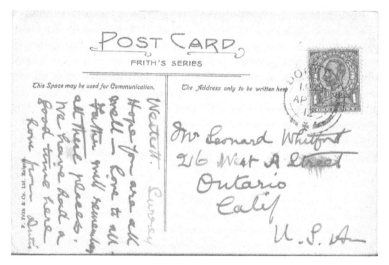

Dorking, Surrey

051315
26 April 1912
Mr Leonard Whitford
216 West A Street
Ontario
California
USA
Westcott, Surrey
Hope you are all well – love to all. Father will remember all these places. We have had a good time here.
Love from Auntie.
Dorking, Surrey

When I was searching for a postcard to illustrate the Mullins' story, I had hoped there would be one of where the family lived in Dorking. Although there are some more recent images, I wasn't able to find one that was suitable. As disappointing as that was, the multi-view of the town and area that I eventually bought from a seller in America proved to be the perfect postcard revealing a parallel story of emigration from England to America.

I found the Whitford family in California in 1910. Samuel Leonard (b.1893), to whom the postcard is addressed, lived with his parents, Samuel and Caroline née Axtens, and two sisters, Irene and Mabel. All the family were born in England and emigrated to America in December 1895. The passenger list shows Samuel as a clerk and in the American census returns he is a gardener.

It wasn't difficult to find the Whitfords before they emigrated. In 1891, they lived in Loughton, Essex and Samuel is listed as a silversmith and secretary to a children's hospital. In 1881, the family lived next door to his parents in London.

Samuel III (b.1852) was a third-generation silversmith – his father and grandfather, both named Samuel, were silversmiths. Samuel's grandfather (b.1781) appears in directories and his work is still available – at a price.

Samuel's father (b.1818) – Samuel II – is listed as employing at least two men, and he was also a secretary to a hospital – in 1871 and 1881. The 1881 census mentions 'the hospital for sick children' – known today as Great Ormond Street Hospital for Children. In 1863 the *British Medical Journal* carried an advert for a series of medical lectures held at the hospital. Tickets were available from Samuel Whitford – confirming a longer association with the hospital than just the period covered by the census returns.

There are a number of examples of Samuel Whitford II being involved in fund-raising for the hospital. An article reproduced on the website for Johns Hopkins University mentions that Samuel was in effect in charge of fund-raising and would give lectures that promoted the hospital's work. He was actively involved in a scheme where cots were sponsored – all helping to support the work of the hospital which had opened in 1852 with only ten beds.

I am indebted to the Archive Service, Great Ormond Street Hospital for Children NHS Foundation Trust for providing me with a copy of a newsletter article about Samuel Whitford and for granting permission for me to include an excerpt:

From the opening of the Hospital for Sick Children at Great Ormond Street in 1852 until 1944, its administrator was known as the Secretary. In the first few months after opening, this was an honorary post held by one of the Board members, but the growing workload meant that a paid post was established in July 1852, to which Samuel Whitford was appointed.

The newsletter mentions that the workload was initially only a few hours a day and this allowed Whitford to continue his work as a silversmith. However, as the hospital developed, so did his workload.

The small scale of the original Hospital and its staff meant that he was effectively also its Treasurer and fundraising manager. Whitford held the post for 32 years, during which he supervised the construction of the first purpose-built Hospital building, and kept the institution out of debt while it led a precariously-funded existence as a charitable Voluntary Hospital. At the time of his retirement, it was estimated that 460,000 patients had used the Hospital during his period in post, and that £400,000 (nearly £20,000,000 at today's values) had passed through his hands as treasurer.

The hospital's archivist was also able to provide examples of Whitford's handwriting – which was greatly affected by his health.

In later years, Whitford was barely able to walk, and he was stricken by what was then called 'Scrivener's Palsy' – his hands effectively crippled by years of writing thousands of letters by hand. He was only able to continue working with the assistance of his son, Samuel junior. Despite the heavy workload at the Hospital, he found time for outside interests, founding and running the Handel Festival Choir and being an active member of the London & Middlesex Archaeological Society. On his retirement in 1884, a photograph of him printed on porcelain (since sadly lost) was given by the clinical staff to hang in the Boardroom.

A Freemason's register from 1893 lists Samuel III working for a children's hospital in Shadwell. This hospital opened in 1868 and, like Great Ormond Street's, received support from Charles Dickens, who, according to the website www.LostLondonHospitals, had visited it twice in 1869.

In later years, Great Ormond Street Hospital benefited from the patronage of another writer, JM Barrie. After graduating from Edinburgh University, Barrie moved to London and lived in lodgings to the rear of Great Ormond Street. He was so affected by the work of the hospital and the plight of children that he gifted the copyright of perhaps his most famous work, *Peter Pan*, to the hospital.

Today, the hospital continues to care for children and its specialist teams are internationally renowned for their skills in treatment, care and research. The hospital's website states that 'every day 618 children and young people arrive at the hospital...' When Dr Charles West opened the hospital in 1852, no one could possibly have imagined that it would become such a centre of excellence.

Although it's not recorded why the Whitford family became involved in the work of children's hospitals, it's possible they were later motivated by the death of Samuel III's seven-year-old brother, Alfred, in 1864. It's also not known why the family emigrated to America nor why Samuel became a gardener.

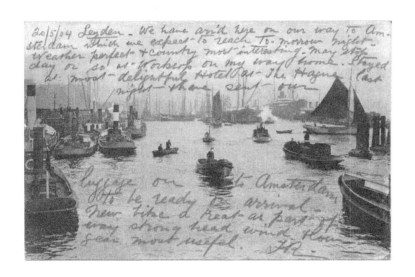

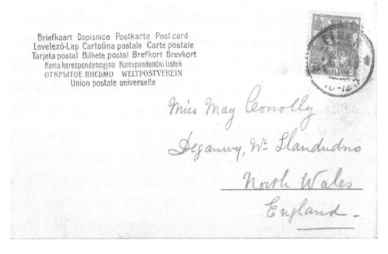

Leiden

052312
20 May 1904
Miss May Conolly
Deganwy
West Llandudno
North Wales
England
We have arrived here on our way to Amsterdam which we expect to reach tomorrow night. Weather perfect and country most interesting – may stop day or so at Worksop on my way home. Stayed at most delightful hotel at The Hague last night and have sent our luggage on to Amsterdam to be ready on arrival – new bike a treat as part of way strong head wind and low gear most useful.
HR

Choosing a postcard that was sent between census years can often be problematic. In the past I've researched postcards where the recipients had moved from the address within weeks of a census being taken – so one that was sent in 1904 could have been a challenge too far.

I began by searching for the recipient by the name on the postcard and failed to find her. But looking further afield and following a few intuitive ideas, led me to a Mary Conolly whose family had links to Wales. I discovered that in other family trees she was known as May. Could she by my May? As I worked on her tree I soon found that her father, John Conolly (b.1861), was living in Deganwy, Llandudno, in 1911. With that piece of the puzzle in place I carried on with (Mary) May Conolly who was born in Birkdale, Lancashire in 1886. Her father, John, was born in Ireland.

In 1901, May was a boarder at a convent school in Rhyl with her sister, Dorothea.

Before the outbreak of the First World War, two of May's brothers emigrated to Canada. George appears in a passenger list of 1911 sailing to Canada as a 16-year-old. He served with the Canadian army during the First World War and was killed in 1917. He is buried in Villers-au-Bois Cemetery in France. The circumstances of his death make hard reading:

When 'going over the top' to capture a machine gun emplacement, he was hit in the head by shrapnel and instantly killed.

Louis emigrated in 1914 and the 1921 census lists his occupation as farmer – and husband to Sybil née Scott who was born in India in 1887. She had emigrated to Canada in 1915. Her father, Major General William Scott, was also born in India and appears in a register of employees with the East India Company in 1896.

Louis and Sybil's son, John (b.1923), was killed during the Second World

War – just a few months after Louis had died in April 1944. Flight Sergeant Conolly's name is included on the Runnymede Memorial at Engleford Green, near Egham:

IN THIS CLOISTER ARE RECORDED THE NAMES OF TWENTY THOUSAND AIRMEN WHO HAVE NO KNOWN GRAVE. THEY DIED FOR FREEDOM IN RAID AND SORTIE OVER THE BRITISH ISLES AND THE LANDS AND SEAS OF NORTHERN AND WESTERN EUROPE

May's eldest brother died in 1947. His probate records confirm that he was the Reverend John Conolly.

Another sibling, Eileen, is listed in 1939 in Wales, living with their mother, Mary née Colbert. Mary was born in Brighton in 1860 and was the daughter of a railway clerk, Michael Colbert, from Wales.

In 1914, May – who received the card – married Francis Kernan from Liscard, Cheshire. (It's worth noting that in some trees he is listed as being born in Liskeard, Ireland. However, the 1911 census, completed by his father, clearly states Liscard, Cheshire.) In 1939, Francis lived in Liverpool as a cotton buyer with daughter Mary (b.1915), who was a secretary to a surgeon. May and Francis had at least three children.

The Pilgrims' journey to America didn't begin with the voyage of the *Mayflower*. In the early 1600s a group seeking religious freedom left England for Holland and settled in Leiden – a city known for tolerance. Instability – including the possibility of war – prompted some of these settlers to consider moving again and they looked to America. The first part of their journey was aboard the *Speedwell* and they sailed from Leiden to Southampton in July 1620.

The 1891 census was the first census to ask a question about the Welsh language in Wales. Many babies less than a year old were recorded as being able to speak Welsh—The National Archives

The West Gate, Southampton

053318
9 September 1909
Miss Katie Collins
231 High Road
Kilburn, London
Dear Katie
Just a card to add to your collection and to show you we have not forgotten you have a PC album. Love to all
Hattie and Alf

In 1911, Katie (Katherine) Collins (b.1903) lived with her parents, Frederick and Harriet née Biggs, and five elder siblings. Frederick was a grocer and sons Frederick, Alfred and Robert were assistants in the business. Elizabeth was a teacher and Gladys and Katie were at school. Although the children were all born in London, Frederick was born in Shirley, Hampshire and Harriet was born in Plumstead, Kent.

Alfred married Henrietta Harriet Harris on Christmas Day 1911. At this time his address is in Heron Road, Willesden. In 1939, the couple lived in Kingston-upon-Thames where he worked as a grocery oilman.

All three sons served in the First World War and Alfred's records are detailed enough to confirm that he served in Italy, Egypt and France. He was injured twice and discharged in 1919. It seems likely that the three brothers all served with the Duke of Cambridge's Own (Middlesex) Regiment. Robert did not survive the war. He was killed in 1917 and is buried in Warlincourt Halte Cemetery, Saulty. His parents' address is listed as Heron Road – confirming, perhaps, that the family had moved shortly after the census of 1911 and before Alfred's marriage.

I briefly considered that the postcard was sent by Alfred and Henrietta Harriet 'Hattie'. However, the writing wasn't a good match for either signature on the marriage register. Also, the card was sent before the couple married. The postcard was sent from Southampton. Shirley – where Frederick was born in 1861 – is part of Southampton. When Frederick and Harriet married in 1885, his father, Francis Collins, was a publican and the family lived at The White Hart in the High Street of Millbrook – another part of Southampton. Did the postcard make its way into Kathy's album? I wonder what happened to the other cards.

West Gate dates back to the 14th century and is one construction that we can say with certainty would have been visible to the passengers of the *Mayflower* and *Speedwell* – and they would have passed through it to reach the dockside. It was built as one of five gateways into the medieval city. It is said that it was through this gate that the army of Henry V marched to the ships for Agincourt in 1415.

The Pilgrim Father Memorial, Southampton

30 November 1913
Mrs Prince
Lynton
Winchester Road, Old Shirley, Southampton
Dear Nell
Just a line to wish you many Happy Returns. Hope you are feeling quite strong by this time.

Sometimes the families I've researched have made it very easy for me to reveal their story – a person in a census may conveniently have been at the same address at the time of their marriage; their father's details might match a mention elsewhere, and so it continues. This isn't one of those cases. I found Ellen Prince with her daughter Florence in 1911. At that time, Ellen is a widow aged 51. In 1901, again with Florence, her age is 41. Going back another ten years and in 1891 Ellen and Florence are with husband Edward Prince and she is recorded as being 52. At this time Edward is 59. In 1881, Ellen's age is recorded as being 45 and Edward is 49. Why was Ellen's age inflated during those years of her marriage?

Edward was born in 1832 and the age difference might have been an embarrassment to the couple – almost 30 years. Once I had confirmed Ellen's maiden name as Staines I was able to accept that her correct year of birth was 1859, meaning that it was only after her husband's death that her correct age was declared – in 1901 and 1911. Given his age when he married Ellen, it's no surprise to discover that Edward had been married before and had other children with his first wife, Jane – William (b.1858) and John (b.1860). Edward's occupation ranged from labourer to musician – a job listed in 1871 and 1881 which spans both families. In earlier years he was a railway worker.

Ellen had at least three sisters – including Flora who was born in 1862. In 1881 she was working in Hampstead as a maid. Her employer was a Professor of Engineering with the University of London. Alexander Kennedy had many interests that included photography and archaeology. He was one of the first to document the site at Petra, Jordan. His work as an engineer possibly affects our lives today – he was involved with the design and construction of generating stations. He was also associated with the electrification of tram systems. We'll never know why Ellen felt it necessary to declare those different ages. Perhaps she didn't even know – after all, it was more likely that the information was provided by her husband without her knowledge. Having a wife the same age as his sons would undoubtably have raised a few eyebrows.

The *Mayflower* and *Speedwell* docked at Southampton for almost two weeks and at least one local man joined the *Mayflower*'s crew at Southampton – cooper John Alden. The memorial was unveiled in 1913.

"Mayflower" Commemorative Stone and Tablet
on the Barbican, Plymouth, England.

The Barbican, Plymouth

154

055274
15 October 1903
Miss Burton
South Street
Exeter
This is very interesting. You will know all about it, I dare say.
Kind regards
WB Bradbury

The Burton family lived in South Street from at least 1881. Edward Burton, who was born in London in 1849, was a cutler and surgical instrument-maker. With wife Harriett née Cave, he had at least three children – Edward Cave Burton, and daughters Grace and Evelyn. All three children were born in Exeter.

In 1909 Grace married George Avent and together the couple ran a stationery and fancy goods shop in London.

We know that the family moved to London after 1903 – when the postcard was sent. Edward senior died in London in 1909 and the 1911 census shows Harriett living in Norwood with Edward and Evelyn. By this time Edward was an insurance clerk and Evelyn is listed as a student of science. She appears in several records as a student, including the University of London where she gained a degree.

Despite the *Speedwell* receiving a refit in Southampton, it continued to leak. After sailing from Southampton both ships were forced to divert to Dartmouth for more work. This was unsuccessful and after sailing on, the ship – with the *Mayflower* – returned to Devon – this time to Plymouth. It became obvious the ship was not seaworthy and would not make the journey across the Atlantic. Its passengers were transferred to the already cramped *Mayflower* and that ship alone carried the Pilgrims, traders and crew to America.

The monument depicted on the postcard is of the Barbican – looking towards the Mayflower Steps. The original steps have long gone but the granite slab with the inscription is believed to be their most likely location.

Plymouth Rock, Plymouth, Massachusetts

056276
10 July 1914
Miss Alice Bragg
Canton
Maine
My dear Alice
This rock on the other side is the one I told you about in school, I stood on it yesterday. I can see the Atlantic Ocean from where I am sitting now. Hope you are having a good time this vacation.
Lovingly
Mary

Although I was never able to trace who sent Alice Bragg her postcard, I do believe Mary has set a scene we can all imagine – sitting near the Rock, gazing out at the Atlantic.

Alice was the youngest of eight children born to Ernest Bragg and Annie née West. Ernest was a farmer and, later, opened a furniture store in Livermore Falls. Three sons appear in census returns as working on farms. The fourth son, Ernest, suffered from ill-health and in every census return as an adult I found him as a patient in a hospital.

Annie West was born in Nova Scotia and in the census returns as a wife, her father's place of birth is given as Scotland. However, in other family trees he is recorded as coming from Ireland. With no documents to check those Irish roots, I was unable to confirm if the US census returns were correct – although it's unlikely Ernest and Annie would have made that mistake.

Ernest's obituary in the *Lewiston Evening Journal* confirms his parents were Thomas and Mary. Thomas Bragg was born in 1834, in Maine. In the 1860 census his job is listed as blacksmith. Later, he appears in records for the American Civil War. He served in the 17th Infantry Regiment Maine and was mustered into service on 27 July 1863 and was killed a year later. According to the register of deaths – a beautifully handwritten ledger that belies its subject – he died of a gunshot wound. Not all the soldiers listed on his page died from battle wounds – smallpox, diarrhoea, pneumonia, typhoid and diphtheria offer an uncomfortable reminder of the conditions the soldiers endured. He is buried in Alexandria National Cemetery in Virginia.

There are some lovely photos of Alice on Ancestry – as a young girl with long ringlets. Alice was born in 1904 and at the time the postcard was sent would have been a pupil at school. Could Mary have been a teacher? Whoever Mary was, Alice kept the postcard and it remains in almost perfect condition.

The memorial depicted on the postcard is a focal point of the *Mayflower* and the story of the Pilgrims. There are suggestions that it was adopted later as the memorial without any firm evidence (within the records of the time) that it is the actual place where the passengers and crew first stepped ashore. Like the memorial in Plymouth, UK, the precise location has been lost.

The Rock was damaged in an attempt to move it – further evidence that the precise position is debatable. Over the years, before it was protected, people are said to have chipped away at the stone, taking their own souvenir.

A minister from England, Henry Allen, was presented with a fragment of the rock during a lecture tour of America in 1883. He took the stone home and it still resides in his church – the Union Chapel, Islington.

The *Mayflower* should never have dropped anchor off the stretch of coastline now known as Plymouth – all those delays in crossing the Atlantic meant that the ship endured storms that delayed it further. It was impossible to continue on to Virginia – some 500 miles away – where there was already an established community.

At Plymouth, there was no shelter and no sanctuary from the squalid conditions of the ship. It would be a year before all the passengers were able to live ashore.

According to the 2016 Census of Canada, the number of Canadians claiming full or partial Scottish descent is 4,799,010.

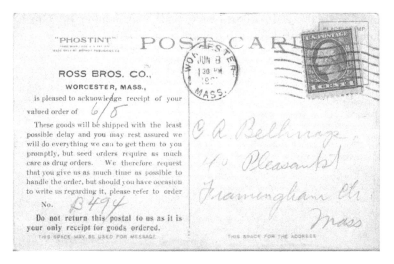

Plymouth in 1622

057300
C R Belknap
40 Pleasant Street
Framingham
Massachusetts

Farmer Comer Belknap (b.1844) lived in Framingham with his wife, Rebecca née Hosmer (b.1846), and their sons, Roscoe and Arthur. As an adult, Roscoe lived at Pleasant Street with his wife, Margaret Balcom, and their children. By this time Roscoe was an accountant.

Arthur moved away from the area and became teacher and dean of a college. He married Mary Blaisdell and the couple and their children lived in Indiana and Pennsylvania.

Rebecca Hosmer's family tree is well documented – she is a member of The Daughters of the American Revolution and her ancestry in that respect is traced back to her great-grandfather Jonathan Ball. He was born in 1751 and enlisted with the Massachusetts militia where he was a private. Other published records show that the Hosmer family emigrated from Hawkhurst, Kent to America in 1635 and settled in Concord.

The image on the card is a depiction of how Plymouth might have looked two years after the arrival of the *Mayflower*. Knowing the hardships of those early settlers – that it was a year before sufficient shelter was available – it's definitely a romanticised view of the area.

Priscilla and John Alden at home

058296
6 June 1907
Miss Cara Armistead
Williamsburg
Virginia
Hello Cara.
Your invitation received. Wish I could have come. Let me congratulate you! I knew you would be valedictorian.
Write sometimes.

Rowland Cara Armistead (b.1890) was the daughter of Cary Armistead and Eudora née Jones. Cary was an attorney who was also the head of the local Democratic party. Cara's success at school stood her in good stead for a career as a teacher (as cited on her death certificate in 1979).

As well as being known for Cary's political and legal career – something continued by Cara's brothers, Cary and Meriwether – the family are still remembered for their part in the development of Colonial Williamsburg. The family lived in Duke of Gloucester Street and their house, built in 1890, was constructed on the site of Charlton's Coffeehouse – an 18th century meeting place where deals were struck and politics debated.

In the 1920s, Colonial Williamsburg, a project funded by John D Rockefeller, set about the reconstruction of the town as it once was. Large areas were bought, buildings demolished and replicas constructed. By this time Cara lived at the family house with her sister, Dora. The sisters refused to sell. A 2020 article published by WYDAILY.com said:

After Cary Peyton Armistead died in 1901, his unmarried daughters, Dora and Cara Armistead, lived in the house while the street around them transformed into colonial history. Throughout their lives, until Dora Armistead died in 1983, the family held onto the property and refused to sell to John D Rockefeller Jr who had torn down all of the structures around them.

In 1985 the Armistead family leased the house to the Association for Preservation of Virginia Antiquities and it became a museum decorated to represent the Victorian-era – something Williamsburg was now lacking. It was later gifted to Colonial Williamsburg and an agreement reached whereby it would not be demolished. Instead, it was decided to relocate the house outside of the colonial area and it was eventually 'wheeled' to its new home.

Once the old site was cleared, the area was excavated and, remarkably, wooden fragments were dated to the colonial era and used in the construction of the 'new' coffeehouse.

Colonial Williamsburg's website makes it clear it's a visitor attraction where one can experience the history of the area. Although those pieces of wood have been included in its construction there doesn't seem much obvious evidence of the coffeehouse's history. The website mentions that some of the brick foundations were original and reused, but the building still looks brand new.

In the UK, we also have these 'living museums' and perhaps the most famous is the Black Country Living Museum which was built on 26 acres of industrial land where some buildings – homes and businesses – have been either built or moved from their original sites.

The Black Country is a heavily industrialised area of the UK in the West Midlands. More than one website attributes the name to the soot produced by the polluting factories. Another suggests the name comes from a thick coal seam that ran near to the surface. My paternal family has its roots in this region – living in and around Oldbury and working in industries that included iron puddling – heavy and dangerous work with a high mortality rate.

How does the Black Country Museum compare to Colonial Williamsburg? Well, it would be almost impossible to construct buildings in wood that appear aged and that perhaps counts against it. In the Black Country Museum, reclaimed bricks add more than a little age and character. This is also true in Colonial Williamsburg. An online video filmed inside the coffeehouse shows a fireplace made from bricks that had been used throughout the building's various lives (albeit not necessarily for the same purpose). It also mentions the meticulous research that led to the wood and paint finishes. I was particularly interested in the bricks. Two kinds had been discovered (defined by colour) and one was confirmed to be from the 1760s. My father, when I was at school, made bricks and the method he used hadn't changed much over the centuries. Bricks were made in Williamsburg using those same methods and the production is now part of the Colonial Williamsburg experience.

What's now known as the Dora Armistead House was added to the National Register of Historic Places in 2020 and is privately owned and being renovated so it can open as an inn. Dora's obituary mentions that Cara had run an overnight lodging house – so the new owners are continuing the house's working history.

With all her family dying within the first year, Priscilla Mullins was alone. But after that first year she married John Alden and together the couple created one of the strongest dynasties of all the *Mayflower* passengers. John became a respected member of the community and an active public servant in Plymouth. The couple and their growing family eventually left Plymouth and settled in the area known today as Duxbury. The list of people who can claim to be direct descendants of John and Priscilla include American presidents, Marilyn Monroe, Dick Van Dyke and Henry Wadsworth Longfellow.

Portland, Maine, Birthplace of Henry W Longfellow
059245

Myles Standish Monument, Duxbury, Massachusetts

060294
10 June 1914
Miss Jennie Boardman
Vineland
New Jersey
Providence, Rhode Island
Dear Cousin Jennie
I am sending you a little token for graduation.
Hope you receive it and do let me know if you do and write and let me know what you are
to do… Love to all from all. Will write letter later.
Lillian

Jennie Boardman, her sisters, brother and parents (George and Carrie née Sullivan) were born in Skowhegan, Maine. By 1910 the family had moved to Vineland, New Jersey where George was a mail carrier. Jennie, who was born in 1894, was a stenographer. In 1923 she worked in Costa Rica where she 'undertook clerical work for the Latin-American Evangelization Campaign'. Her passport application confirms she needed the passport for missionary work. An online document (A short history of the Latin American Biblical University By Alvaro Perez, Librarian As translated by UBL Professor Ruth Mooney) provided some information about Jennie's work. The campaign began in Great Britain in the mid-19th century and in 1922 a training school for women was opened and in 1923 (matching the dates Jennie left America) 93 were enrolled. It could be that Jennie was one of the first group of women. Apart from this document I didn't find much more that linked Jennie to the campaign. By 1930 she was back with her family in New Jersey.

Captain Myles (Miles) Standish was a military officer employed to organise the protection of the Pilgrims in their new home. He would remain in Plymouth and then help found the nearby town of Duxbury with other settlers who moved away – perhaps because of the strict religious practices of the Pilgrims.

Standish was immortalised in American poet Henry Wadsworth Longfellow's poem: *The Courtship of Miles Standish*. The poem tells the story of Standish's unrequited love for Priscilla Mullins whose heart was taken by John Alden. Written centuries after the event, it's a fictionalised account of relationships blossoming in the new country. Standish lived into his seventies and died in Duxbury.

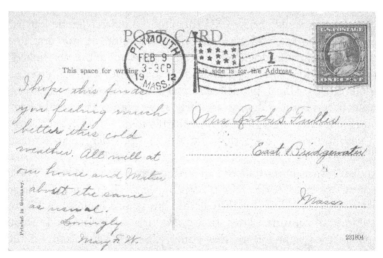

Old Department Store, Duxbury, Massachusetts

061303
9 February 1912
Mrs Ruth S Fuller
East Bridgewater
Massachusetts
I hope this finds you feeling much better this cold weather.
All well at our home and Mother about the same as usual.
Lovingly
May FW

Ruth Fuller née Upman appears in official records with a number of alternative spellings for her maiden name. I've chosen to use Upman from the records filed for her marriage to John Fuller, a farmer who was born in 1821. Ruth was born in 1828 and the couple married in Bridgewater, Massachusetts in 1849. Ruth's father was a naturalised American citizen who was born in Italy. Antonio died in 1876 and is buried in the Mayflower Cemetery with his wife, Rebecca née Chandler, who was born in Duxbury. In the 1870 census, at the age of 76, Antonio worked in an iron works.

Not content with its connections to the passengers of the *Mayflower*, Duxbury was also home to the Ford Store. Established in 1826, Ford's is believed to be the first department store in America. In 1921 it was damaged by fire – known for using kerosene and wood stoves for heating, it was perhaps an accident waiting to happen. Today, there is a marker outside the original location on Tremont Street, put in place in 1937.

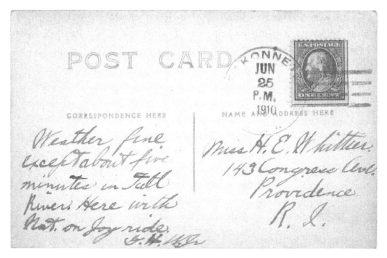

Betty Alden House, Littlecompton, RI

062298
25 June 1910
Miss HE Whittier
143 Congress Avenue
Providence
RI
Weather fine except about five minutes in Fall River.
Here with Nat on joy ride.

In 1910 Hope Whittier lived with her parents, Henry and Fannie née Northup. Henry was a diamond jeweller and his son from his first marriage, Ira, would continue the family business.

Henry served in the Civil War and enlisted in 1862 at the age of 18. At this time he was already a jeweller. Less than a year later he was discharged with a disability.

Ira married Nellie Tanner in 1887. Nellie's father was a cigar-maker – as was her brother George. Another brother, Christopher, worked with Ira – his brother-in-law – and their business appears in several trade directories as Whittier & Tanner from 1908 to 1947.

Hope, who received the card, married Ernest Anderson, a bank worker.

The Betty Alden House is an important monument in the story of the Pilgrims. She is known as the first-born daughter of the Pilgrims – a title attached to her in 1891 by American novelist Jane G Austin. Of course, it can't be proven if this is correct. As the first child born to Priscilla and John Alden, Betty was born in 1623–4 and it seems unlikely that no other girls were born before this time – although not impossible. With her husband, William Peabodie, she had 13 children and it was in their later years they moved to Little Compton. Like Betty's father, her husband was also involved in the governing of their town.

063302
20 November 1910
Mrs JJ Reed
Pillow
Dauphin County
Pennsylvania
Dear Aunt Addie
A Happy Thanksgiving to all. This is a fine day. We expect get guests over Thanksgiving.
Our parsonage is about completed, it is very nice. Come and see us when we are in it.
Lovingly Nora

Adelaide Bassler (b.1845) married Dr Jesse Reed in 1879. The couple had at least one child, Henry, who would also become a doctor. Adelaide was the daughter of Reverend Henry (Henrich) Bassler (b.1804) and Rebecca née Dechant (b.1811). According to local history records that are available online, Henry and the family lived in Dauphin and he was 'the first pastor of Christ Church and preached his last sermon in the German language on May 12, 1839'. Adelaide was one of at least 11 children and several brothers served in the Civil War, including Albert who was killed in 1866 and is remembered on the Millersburg Civil War memorial.

Adelaide's husband, Dr Jesse Reed, also served in the Civil War. He was mustered into service at Harrisburg as a private. After the war he trained at Philadelphia's Jefferson Medical College. With his first wife, Catharine Leinbach, he had at least five children and of those I traced, Arthur became a linguist and Jay a teacher.

Who was Nora? I didn't find her – many of Adelaide's siblings had very little supporting documents and it wasn't possible to confirm them beyond appearances as children with their parents.

The idea of celebrating Thanksgiving is closely associated with the Pilgrims – giving thanks for their first successful harvest. Other areas of America lay claim to celebrating the true 'first' Thanksgiving – including at Berkeley Hundred in Charles City County in Virginia where there is a shrine built for its commemoration of the 1619 event. There's no doubt that the first one celebrated in Plymouth was of huge importance and led to the hope that their fragile community could survive.

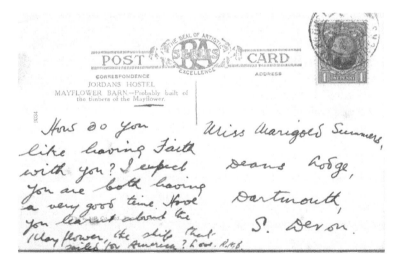

Mayflower Barn, Jordans Hostel

064301
1935
Miss Marigold Summers
Dean's Lodge
Dartmouth
South Devon
How do you like having Faith with you? I expect you are both having a very good time.
Have you learnt about the Mayflower, the ship that sailed for America?
Love. RK.B.

Marigold was born in Leeds in 1926 and her father, Percy (b.1889), was a lecturer. In 1911, he is listed as a mining student and his father, Henry, was a merchant selling oil, colour [paint] and groceries. Henry's probate records from 1928 confirm that Percy was a metallurgist and his brother, Charles, was a civil servant. When Charles died his address is given as the Dean's Lodge.

Henry, Marigold's grandfather, married Esther Barton in 1883. Her father was a butcher and after his death, her mother, also Esther, continued the work and is recorded in 1881 as being a butcher and dairy keeper and employed one man and one boy. Her son, Charles, is also at the address, working as an oil and colour merchant.

Marigold appears in passenger lists with her father. They sailed first class from South Africa, arriving at Plymouth – which is a lovely connection to the message on the postcard.

Jordans is a small village in Buckinghamshire and is perhaps best known as the burial site of William Penn, founder of Pennsylvania. It's also known as a centre for Quakerism and home to the Mayflower Barn – said to have been partly constructed from the ship's beams. Although it is recorded that beams from a ship were used in its construction (in the 17th century), it cannot be proven these came from the *Mayflower* (or that they didn't). It's worth considering that at the time the *Mayflower* ceased work, the ship had no historical importance and is unlikely to have been of sufficient interest to have been taken from where she was broken up. Only later would the name *Mayflower* become synonymous with the Pilgrims.

As this section about the *Mayflower* and her passengers draws to its conclusion, I'd like to believe that the beams are from the *Mayflower* and that a little part of her remains in the old country.

HEAVEN ON EARTH.

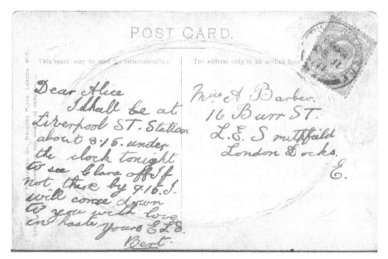

Heaven on Earth

065327
11 December 1911
Miss A Barber
16 Burr Street
LE Smithfield
London Docks
Dear Alice
I shall be at Liverpool Street Station about 8.15 under the clock tonight to see Clara off.
If not there by 9.15 I will come down to you.
With love in haste.
Yours
ELS
Bert

In 1913, Alice Barber married Albert Shepherd and I was delighted to see that his signature matched Bert's on the card.

Alice was the daughter of engineer Walter Barber and his wife, Martha née Chew. In some records he is listed as a brewer's steam engineer. The family lived at the address on the postcard for decades – from at least 1891.

At the time of his marriage to Alice, Bert was a blacksmith. At other times his job is given as a gas stove fitter. It might be that he worked with his father, James, who is listed as a gas engineer and gas meter prover – testing their accuracy. In 1939, he is listed again as a blacksmith.

Who was Clara?

In 1921, Bert witnessed the marriage of Clarence Longman and Clara Barber – Alice's sister. Widower Clarence was a shirt manufacturer and in some records he appears as a hosiery and fancy draper's shop owner. His parents were Charles Longman and (his second wife), Clara née Atterbury – and just to confirm how confusing some trees are, Clarence had a sister, Clara.

Clara Atterbury (Clarence's mother) was the daughter of a shoemaker and she married Charles Longman on Christmas Day, 1869 – a rare non-working day.

With his first wife, Adelaine née Ball, Clarence had two children – Clarence and Adelaine.

Who was the Clara in the postcard? The ages of the Claras in the extended tree suggest it could be Alice's sister – although the idea that Alice would not be aware of her sister leaving on an evening train and being seen off by Bert is a conundrum I can never hope to solve. The habit of keeping a name alive throughout the generations is a common one in most family trees. Bert and Alice did this with their daughter, Doris Clara, who was born in 1914.

Haydn Sailing to England

066324
Miss K Farrow
Eaglehurst
Wisbech
Good luck –
Best wishes and dear love.
G
30.11.11

Kate Farrow was born in 1876 and was one of seven children. In 1911 she was a music teacher and lived with her mother, Jane née Freeth (who was born in Weston, Somerset), and three siblings. Apart from sister Edith, who was born in Norfolk, the children were born in Wisbech.

Their father, Henry Farrow, had died shortly before the 1911 census had been taken and he was a builder – listed in one return as employing 12 men and four boys. Henry was born in Fulmodeston, Norfolk.

In 1871, Henry was a carpenter joiner and his father, Robert Farrow (b.1797), was a publican in Norfolk. In 1851 Robert is listed as innkeeper of The Star in Barney Road, Fulmodeston.

From 1854 until his death in 1871, he was the publican of The Ship Inn in Gaywood. After his death, the pub was run by his widow, Sarah née Garner. Later, after a break of a few months, their son, Edward, would take on the business until 1883. According to the website www.NorfolkPubs, The Ship Inn had a small theatre and was 'frequented by travelling players' – although it's not clear if this happened during the Farrow family's time which spanned almost 30 years.

Kate's career as a music teacher was a long one – in 1939 she is still living and working in Wisbech. Two sisters were also teachers. Mabel worked in a private school in Goole, Yorkshire. Gertrude also worked in a private school – in Clifton Crescent, Folkstone – making it very likely that she, Gertrude, is the G who sent the postcard. With Kate's musical background, the sending of a card (albeit a gloomy one) depicting the composer Haydn is apt – although we can't know about what Gertrude wished her luck.

Kate and Gertrude lived long lives – Gertrude passed 100 years and Kate missed out by only a few months. The family's connection with Eaglehurst continued until at least the 1950s when Mabel died.

Many Happy Returns.

May all thy hours be winged with Joy.
Byron.

POST CARD

Dear Nellie

Just a line to wish

You very "many Happy returns

of the Day" with love.

Florrie.

Miss N. Plant
583 Holloway Road
Upper Holloway
N.

Byron

067326
Miss N Plant
583 Holloway Road
Upper Holloway
Dear Nellie
Just a line to wish you very 'Many Happy returns of the Day'.
With love
Florrie

Nellie Plant was the youngest daughter of butcher Arthur Plant and his wife, Mary née Reeve. She was born in 1897 and her sister, Maud, two years earlier.

The family lived at a different address in 1901, but still within the St Pancras, Holloway area of London. Although Arthur Plant and his seven siblings were all born in London, their parents, John Plant and Dinah née Skinner, were from Lincolnshire.

I found John in Kirton, Lincolnshire in 1861, with his first wife Susannah née Stow, working as a butcher. Dinah Skinner, who was born in Leake, was working for the family as a domestic. At this time her age is given as 20 – making her year of birth 1841 and this is confirmed by her birth and baptism records.

The Plant family appears in several online trees and one researcher has added information about John's business. In 1863, after the death of Susannah, local papers indicated his financial plight by advertising the sale of his property to clear his debts prior to him being declared bankrupt.

Shortly after this, John and Dinah relocated to London and married in 1864. At the time of the marriage they are living at separate addresses in the Holloway area and Dinah is unable to sign her name.

By 1871 they have four children and Dinah's age has increased by eight years, giving her a revised year of birth of 1833. This year was used to calculate her age on the next two census returns. John changed career during these years and became a decorator.

After John's death in 1899, the 1901 census shows Dinah's age as matching her birth records. Similarly, in 1911, when as the head of the household she completes the 1911 census, she uses her correct age. This follows through into her death records in 1912.

Did she know that John was misrepresenting her age? Was 20 years considered too big a difference? Undoubtedly the family were verging on the notorious side in Lincolnshire – bankruptcy and a relationship with a live-in domestic was left behind. Why not the age difference?

Anyone who has ever had to check handwritten documents will know that errors creep into transcriptions but we should never assume that the information provided for the census returns is correct. This story is a reminder that there are tangled webs in the corner of many family histories.

068334
13 July 1911
Master Sidney Holness
'Rose Hotel'
High Street
Deal
Dear Sidney
To wish you many Happy Returns of the Day.
Grannie is so sorry she did not send yours till today. Better late than never.
With all good wishes from Uncle Tom.
Grannie is very well.

Young Sidney was the son of Richard Holness and Rosanna née Philpott and was born in Broadstairs, Kent in 1897. Richard and Rosanna were born in Ramsgate. It would be lovely to think the Rose Hotel was named after Rosanna, but that's not the case.

According to the hotel's current website, it has been a 'significant landmark on Deal's High Street for over 200 years'. The website has some wonderful images of the hotel and continues with: 'In the Victorian and Edwardian era The Rose was one of the town's most popular venues for smokers, evening entertainments and posh dinners'.

In 1901, the Holness family lived at The Swan in Queen Street, Deal. The website dover-kent.com has photos of the pub taken just after the Holness family had moved on. In 1938 the building was demolished and replaced by another pub of the same name.

Who sent the postcard? Rosanna's brother, Tom Philpott, lived, at the time of the postcard, with their parents in Ramsgate. Tom was a butcher and their father, Sidney Philpott, was a gardener. Grannie was Mary née Tottman.

Sidney served in the First World War as a gunner in the Machine Gun Corps.

Children's Corner, Scarborough

069336
19 August 1911
Miss C Butterworth
29 Cromwell Grove
Levenshulme
Having a good time.
Wish you were here.
I suppose you are seeing a lot during the strike but do not get injured with the bricks etc.
Flo

Constance Butterworth was born in 1890 in Bacup, Lancashire. For a number of years her father, Joseph Butterworth (b.1854), was a draper and by 1911 he was an inspector for an insurance company. Two brothers, Granville and Joseph, would become teachers.

All the family, including their mother, Fanny née Taylor, were born in Bacup, Lancashire – 30 miles from Levenshulme. Florence – Flo – who likely sent the postcard, was a manageress in a fancy drapery store.

According to his probate records from 1861, Constance's paternal grandfather, James Butterworth, was a power loom weaver. The census return of that year lists his widow, Ruth née White, as a cotton weaver. At only 29 she also had three young children to care for. Ten years later only Joseph is living at home – and also working as a weaver. Later, he married and started his own family, working as a draper.

Constance became a shorthand typist for a rubber works. Quite possibly this might have been David Moseley and Sons who had a factory less than three miles away. The company was founded in 1833 and became involved in the production of components used in the telephone industry.

Betws-y-Coed

070337
31 December 1903
Miss Bessie Miles
16 Bramhall St.
Warrington
CC Happy. New. Year.
Maggie

Bessie Miles was born in Warrington in 1886 and was one of five children born to William Miles and Lois née Currier. Although the children were born in Lancashire, William was born in Walsall, in the West Midlands, and Lois in Swinton, Yorkshire.

In 1911 William is listed as a shingler for an iron manufacturer – hammering puddled iron. In 1871 the family are in Swinton and he is a helper in a rolling mill – possibly working with his father, also William, who is a mill furnace man along with another son, Thomas.

In 1901, Bessie is listed as a teacher's candidate – employed within a school at the age of 15. She married soap-cooler Edgar Hayward in 1910.

Bessie's sister, Gladys, is listed in 1911 as working as an operator with the National Telephone Company. The company traded for 30 years and was taken over by the General Post Office in 1912.

Off St Kilda

071352
3 September 1904
Mrs C Evans
High Street
Timsbury
Near Bath
31 Shadwell Road
Bishopston
Dear Aunt
Glad to say we arrived home quite safe about 8pm.
I am glad to have had the pleasure of seeing you all.
Thanks for all kindness shown to us.
Yours ever
EMG

Ann Evans née Flower was born in Timsbury, Somerset in 1834 to parents John and Elizabeth.

In 1853 she married Charles Evans, a farmer from Timsbury, and the couple had ten children, including five sons.

In 1911, John was a carpenter living in Horfield, Bristol with his wife Ellen. Their daughter Annie was a packer in a chocolate factory and sons John and Walter were tramway conductors. The postcard used to illustrate the next story must surely have been a view familiar to John and Walter.

Another son, Percy, went to America in 1913. Although Percy Evans appears in several overseas records, only one has a proven link to the Horfield address. Charles, another son, became a butcher in Hedge End, Hampshire.

Jacob became a despatching clerk and in 1911 lived in Deptford, London with his India-born wife Florence Haig.

In 1911 Thomas is listed as a rural postman in Timsbury – suggesting he stayed closer to home. However, his children were born in Oxfordshire and his wife, Amy Brayfield, was born in Newcastle-under-Lyme and the couple married in Hartshill, Stoke-on-Trent.

Who sent the card? Ann Flower's sister, Eliza (b.1819), had at least five children with her husband, James Ford. Ellen Mary Ford married James Gould, an insurance agent from Downside, Somerset – giving us the initials EMG.

The Tramway Centre, Bristol

072264
23 August 1912
Mrs T Williams
Hamptworth
Redlynch
Near Salisbury
Wiltshire
Dear Rose
Many thanks for photo. Isn't it splendid and Maurice, he looks such a jolly little chap and he has grown since I saw him last. Have you got Reggie back yet. Not very nice weather for them. It is nothing else but rain here.
Much love to you all.
Nellie

The postcard addressed to Rose Williams née Russen was sent to her by her sister Nellie. In 1911, Nellie was a servant working in Ryde, Isle of Wight – from where the card was posted.

Rose married Thomas Williams in 1901 in Pluckley, Kent. A few months later the couple worked as caretaker and gardener at Sherland House, Pluckley. Rose was born in 1879 in Brockenhurst, and Thomas was born in Redlynch, Wiltshire four years earlier.

In 1911, they lived with Thomas' mother, Eliza née Andrews, at the beer house in Hamptworth. The family had lived at the address since at least 1871 and Eliza's husband, James, who died in 1898, is listed as a beer retailer and grocer. In 1901, Eliza, as head of the household, is listed as a grocer and her son, James junior, is the seller of beer.

There's a pub in the village today – The Cuckoo. Although it's unclear when it was officially named, it was done so during the time the Williams family ran it – confirmed by Thomas' probate records from 1937.

Various websites describe The Cuckoo as a picturesque early 18th century inn. It's relatively small compared with today's purpose-built pubs. The 1911 census confirms it had seven rooms.

Nellie Russen, who sent her sister the card, married carpenter Thomas Gillen and the couple eventually lived in Southampton.

The postcard's message mentions Maurice – Rose and Thomas' youngest son who was born in 1910. Rose's probate records show that Maurice became a local government officer.

Maori Cooking at Hot Springs, New Zealand

073353
31 May 1915
Mr GF Wray
~~*Cloughton*~~
~~*Scarborough*~~
~~*Yorks*~~
Court Alum
Alumhurst Road
Bournemouth
England
Thank you very mutch [sic] *for card. Glad to hear your was keeping well as we are all well. We have had the first fall of snow today 31 May.*
With kind regards from us all.
HS

This postcard travelled around the world and across the UK and the story behind its journey is just as well-travelled.

George Wray was born in Bainton, Yorkshire in 1881. In 1901, his family lived at The Hall, Cloughton. His grandfather, William Wray (b.1817), was a clergyman and George's father, Herbert Wray (b.1852), was 'financially independent'.

In 1911, George's parents and sisters, Helen and Cicely, were on holiday in Lyndhurst, Hampshire – not far from where the postcard was eventually redirected to in Bournemouth (now in Dorset, but Hampshire at this time).

George served in the First World War as a captain and in his retirement lived in Preston, Weymouth, Dorset with his uncle, Charles Medcalf (his mother Amy Medcalf's brother). Charles was vicar of the local parish church. Sister Helen also moved to Dorset and died in Preston.

George had one brother – Maurice. He left the UK for a number of years and lived in Costa Rica with his wife, Colina Campbell, where he grew coffee. Their only son, Michael, was killed in an accident in the army in 1947 and is buried in Germany. Maurice and Colina eventually moved to Bridport, Dorset.

Who had sent the postcard? Well, I didn't expect to find the sender as a relative of George's – given the style and formality in the message. But a clue came from George's sister Cicely. In 1914 she married George Doe, the son of a solicitor from Great Torrington, Devon. He lived in Oroua, New Zealand in 1911. Many of the Wray family appear in passenger lists sailing to and from England and it's possible that George Wray knew George Doe and was in New Zealand for a while. Unfortunately it isn't possible to read the New Zealand cancellation mark – had it read Oroua I would have been very pleased to confirm the connection!

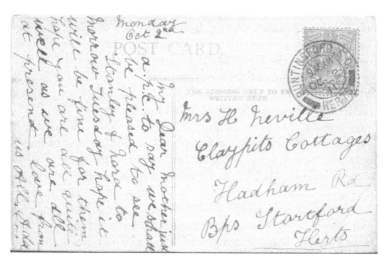

Greenwich Hospital

074354
2 October 1911
Mrs H Neville
Claypits Cottages
Hadham Road
Bishop's Stortford
Hertfordshire
My Dear Mother
Just a PC to say we shall be pleased to see Stanley and Nora tomorrow Tuesday. Hope it will be fine for them. Hope you are all quite well as we are all at present.
Love from us All
Ada
XXXX

Henry Neville and Sarah née Bush were born in Henham, Essex. Henry was a labourer and they married in 1876 and had ten children.

Ada, who sent the postcard, was born in 1881 and married William Rayment, a leather cutter from Sandon, Hertfordshire.

Stanley, who Ada mentions in her message, was a railway labourer and later became a capstan attendant. He married Leonora Nash – Nora – who, in 1901, was a servant working in a training college for schoolmistresses in Bishop's Stortford.

Another brother, Jesse, was a locomotive driver. His wife, Ellen née Middleditch, was a chocolate packer. In 1939 their son, Harold, was a laboratory assistant with the Royal Arsenal. He would later move to Weymouth, Dorset and his mother died nearby in Dorchester.

Considering how many children Henry and Sarah had – ten – it was frustratingly difficult to find out too much about each child beyond a job title. Ada and William also had a large family – eight children with four dying before 1911. There was also little available about them – a reminder that the census returns and other online records only reveal certain facts. Consider your own story if it were only defined by the census returns.

Ellen quite possibly worked in the Menier chocolate factory (built in the 1870s) – it was certainly near to where she lived. The large building in Southwark eventually became derelict but was rescued and transformed into what is now an arts complex and theatre.

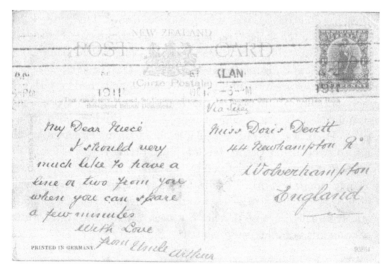

Whakarewarewa Bridge, New Zealand

075355
1911
Via Suez
Miss Doris Devitt
44 Newhampton Road
Wolverhampton
England
My Dear Niece
I should very much like to have a line or two from you when you can spare a few minutes.
With love
From
Uncle Arthur

Doris Devitt was born in 1896 and was one of seven children born to butcher George Devitt and Rosa née Asbury. George was the son of Ireland-born poulterer John Devitt who ran a business in Wolverhampton.

Two of Doris' sisters – Marie and Kathleen – became schoolteachers. Brothers Leslie and Dennis were railway clerks – as was Doris. Gordon and Alan were also clerks. Alan served in the RAF during the First World War and was killed in April 1918 in France. He is remembered on the Arras Flying Services Memorial as Second Lieutenant Alan Devitt. The memorial is in the Faubourg-d'Amiens Cemetery, Arras and commemorates almost 1000 airmen of the Royal Naval Air Service, the Royal Flying Corps and the Royal Air Force who have no known grave.

Doris' uncle – Arthur Asbury – appears in records in New Zealand from 1902 where he was a government clerk. He is mentioned in newspaper reports as a deputy returning officer in elections held in the November of that year. He died in Auckland in 1927.

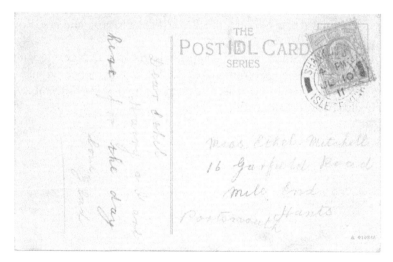

The Old Village, Shanklin, Isle of Wight

076357
10 July 1911
Miss Ethel Mitchell
16 Garfield Road
Mile End
Portsmouth
Hampshire
Dear Ethel
Harry and I are here for the day.
Love Glad

Ethel Mitchell was born in 1888 and was one of nine children born to Thomas Mitchell and Jane née Pennell. Ethel's parents were born in Sherborne and Warminster, respectively. At one time, Thomas was a corporation road sweeper. In the 1911 census Ethel and her sister Emily were sewing machinists making corsets.

Thomas Mitchell's parents were William and Hannah née Buglar. William was born in Sherborne, Dorset in 1789 and Hannah was born in Thornford, a village not far from Sherborne, in 1788. At the time of their marriage in 1822, neither could sign their name.

In 1861, William and Hannah lived in Acreman Street in Sherborne. Hannah worked as a silk winder and it's no surprise that on the same page ten other women were involved in the silk industry. A few minutes' walk from Acreman Street finds the town's silk factory (now redeveloped into small business units).

In 1861 almost 600 people were employed in the mill. After a decline there was a resurgence in the business when it was commissioned to produce silk for Queen Victoria's Diamond Jubilee. It's possible that the Mitchells lived in a home built by the silk factory – although some records suggest the main building of these homes didn't commence until 1861.

Ten years later, when the couple were in their 80s, they had moved into the town's almshouses to the side of Sherborne Abbey. Today, this building, like the abbey, has become a tourist attraction. However, it still cares for the elderly – but with a much more modern and comfortable ambience. An article by Colin Trueman in *Dorset Life* from 2012 outlines some of the rules from 1862 that William and Hannah endured:

> *'...to promote the welfare of its inmates and particularly their due preparation for the hour of Death, and for the day of Judgement, according to the pious intent of the founder...' and also require the 'poor men', 'poor women', 'Housewife' and 'feeble inmates of either sex' to attend 'Divine Service in the Chapel... in the morning at 7 o'clock and in the evening at 9 o'clock from Lady-day to Michaelmas, and in the morning at 8 o'clock and in the evening at 7 o'clock from Michaelmas to*

Lady-day…' In addition, the 'poor men and women shall continue to attend the Public Worship of Almighty GOD as heretofore, going and returning two and two in good order, according to the custom of this house…'

As well as Ethel's father, Thomas, the couple had another son, William. He married Matilda Manley from Bridport in 1842. Their son, Albert, who was born in Southampton in 1849, would also know hardship.

There are few records of Albert available and the one I found tells a sad story. He last appears in the census returns in the UK in 1861 with his parents and siblings in Bristol where his father was a coach-maker. The next sighting of him in official records is his death certificate in Yuma, Arizona in 1934 – at the age of 85.

The cause of death is given as pneumonia. He had lived to what might be considered a good age – but it's the other details that suggest great hardship. He had arrived in Arizona only a week earlier and died in a transient camp in December. He was recorded as an unmarried prospector. Although he had only been in Arizona for a week, the death certificate confirms that he first arrived in America when he was 20. Unusually there was no trace of him in passenger lists (two possible sightings only gave the name with no other information that could be used). His death certificate includes the details of both parents, including his mother's maiden name – and his place of birth as South Hampton [sic].

Whatever possible adventures he found in America, there's no doubt his ending was a sad one. His grave in the Yuma Pioneer Cemetery is marked with a rough piece of stone, possibly granite. It bears only his name and dates of birth and death.

The Yuma Pioneer Cemetery was established in May 1895. Today, local volunteers work to preserve the headstones – and the history of the region.

Gibraltar – entrance to the harbour

077358
21 April 1910
Mrs MJ Huggins
7 Buller Street
Carlton Road
Derby
Thanks for letter. Very pleased that you had so many remembrances. Sorry that I do not feel quite alright. Hope the warmer weather will make me better. Very fine here today.
Love to both
Clem

Matthew Huggins and Betsy Liddiard were married in 1893 in Harewood, Yorkshire. Before they married, Betsy was a teacher in Broome, Worcestershire where she lived with her younger sister, Kate. In 1881 Betsy was a pupil-teacher in Tetford, Lincolnshire – not far from where she was born. The census return for this year shows she is a boarder with the Rawlinson family whose daughter, Celia, was also a pupil-teacher.

At the time Betsy married Matthew, she doesn't record an occupation. However, Matthew was a teacher and over the following years the couple lived in Derbyshire and Staffordshire where he worked. During the First World War, Matthew served in the RAF, enlisting in 1918 when he was 49.

The postcard was sent by Matthew's sister, Clementina. Like her brother, she was born in Gloucestershire. Clementina worked for bookseller and printer William Clee who, with his wife Ann, ran a shop in the High Street, Cheltenham. After they retired, Clementina continued to work in the business and still lived with the couple away from the town centre. They had no children, so perhaps that explains why Clementina lived with them for so many years – at least from 1881 to 1911. The mention of 'remembrances' would seem to refer to Betsy's April birthday.

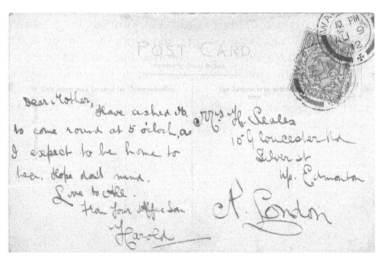

The Mill Pond, Swanage

078365
9 August 1912
Mrs H Seales
159 Gloucester Road
Silver Street
Edmonton
London
Dear Mother
Have asked M to come round at 5 o'clock as I expect to be home to tea.
Hope don't mind.
Love to all
From your affectionate son
Harold

Harold Seales was a carpenter – as were his father, Arthur, and brother, Herbert. Later, Harold would become a grocer and in the 1930s he lived with his wife just around the corner from the address on this postcard.

Harold and Herbert were born in Enfield, but their parents were born in Norfolk and Suffolk in 1863 – Esther née Aldrich in Elmham and Arthur in Corton, where his family ran The White Horse pub. Esther's father was a miller as was her brother, David. The family lived in Silver Street from at least 1901 and Esther was at the address when she died in 1935.

Esther's sister, Alice Aldrich, married Alfred Osborne in 1884. The couple lived in Great Yarmouth and their 1911 census return is very detailed as to his occupation:

'Foreman for Lowestoft Water and Gas Company at Lound Water Works'. Alfred also records his duties: 'superintending of new boiler houses and filters and making of new storage basins and working of filters and general work of grounds'.

Harold, who sent the postcard, served in the First World War and his records reveal that he was 5' 3" tall and had a fair complexion.

In 1917 Harold married May Wraight. She was born in Clapton in 1895 and worked as a buttonhole and collar hand. Her father, Vincent, was a clerk. He and May's mother, Ellen née Ripsher, had 14 children and two of their daughters, Ellen and Grace, worked filling cartridges in an ammunition factory. In 1911 the family lived in Folkestone Road, Edmonton – not far from Eley Brothers – a manufacturer of ammunition.

Might May be the person Harold had invited for tea? I do hope so. The couple lived near to each other, at least in 1911.

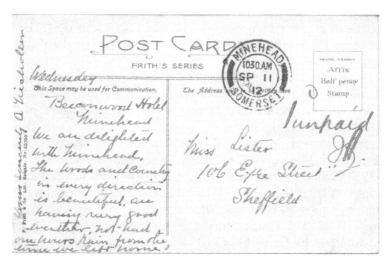

Selworthy Almshouses

079360
11 September 1912
Miss Lister
106 Eyre Street
Sheffield
Wednesday
Beaconwood Hotel
Minehead
We are delighted with Minehead, the woods and country in every direction is beautiful, are having very good weather, not had one hour's rain from the time we left home.
Yours sincerely A Nicholson

Helen Lister's family lived in Eyre Street from at least the 1830s. Her mother, Sarah, ran a carrier business and most of her nine children continued this business at a number of addresses in Eyre Street – numbers 60, 62, 104 and 106. Helen, who received the card, was the youngest child that I traced and was born in Sheffield in 1827. Helen's eldest sibling was Ann who was born in 1805.

When she died in 1914, Helen was still living in Eyre Street. This part of Sheffield is known for its cutlery and manufacturing industries and it's likely that the family were involved in conveying the products around the country. One advert mentions them being carriers to Birmingham.

Over the years the buildings in Eyre Street have been demolished, replaced and cleared again to make way for wider roads and even a multi storey car park. There are photographs online of how the street once looked with factories producing gardening tools, cutlery and general knives. Across the way were gold and silver refining works, rolling mills and other associated businesses. Butler's Cutlery had their works at number 105 but began trading in 1768 in nearby Trinity Street. In 1850 the company was taken over and relocated to Eyre Street in 1864 – when the Listers were living in the street. This new company ceased trading in the 1950s but the name lives on having been bought by Arthur Price in 1993.

Despite this being an industrialised area, other families lived in the street. The postcard was possibly sent to Helen by a near neighbour – Elizabeth Nicholson (b.1853). Elizabeth lived at number 122 Eyre Street with one of her three children, Charles, who was a plasterer. The family, like the Listers, lived in Eyre Street for a number of years and were there from at least 1891. At that time, Elizabeth's husband was alive. John Nicholson was also a plasterer and was born in 1850. In 1911, Elizabeth was employed as a spring knife 'wetter'. As head of the household she had completed the census return – offering a relatively good match to the handwriting on the card. Unfortunately, as the card was signed 'A Nicholson' there remains a question over who actually sent it.

A guidebook from around the time A Nicholson visited Minehead reveals something of the hotel:

...beautifully situated in its own Private Grounds... and commands the most extensive and lovely range of woodland scenery... There is... *electric light throughout, Billiards, a Tennis Lawn... it is a first class Family Hotel.*

It was interesting to see that there is also a feature about Selworthy and the almshouses. The view in the guidebook is the one used in the postcard – perhaps that is why they chose it.

In 1911, one man described an occupant of his house as 'Peter Tabby' and lists his occupation as 'mouser'. His nationality is 'Persian'. The enumerator has crossed out the entry with red ink and noted sternly: 'This is a cat'—The National Archives

The new GPO – King Edward Building

080366
19 December 1918
London
Miss D Peters
No. 68 Bancroft Road, Mile End, London
Dear Sister Daisy
Many thanks for the stamps which I received on Thursday morning. The visitors are allowed to come in the ward on Christmas Sunday and Boxing day but I don't know about afterward.
Best love and kisses from your loving sister

Daisy Peters lived with her siblings William and Elizabeth, and their widowed mother, Elizabeth née Thornton. Despite having the family at the address on the card in 1911, they proved an elusive project to research.

In 1903, Daisy was baptised in St Simon Zelotes church in Bethnal Green, London. Fortunately, the register also includes her date of birth (21 March 1903) – and her parents' names of William and Elizabeth. Just that information alone isn't sufficient to prove this is the Daisy on the postcard. However, the family's address is given as 68 Bancroft Road and William's occupation, a gunmaker.

Elizabeth was baptised on Christmas Eve in 1899 and her birth is recorded as 1 December. At this time the family lived in Great Camberley Street and were at that address when William was baptised in 1898 (born 13 July).

Is there any proof that Elizabeth and William are Daisy's sister and brother? William's baptism records confirm his father was a gunmaker. The marriage register for their parents shows that in 1897 Elizabeth lived in Great Camberley Street – and that the William she married was a gunmaker. It also confirmed that their fathers (both named William) were a cabinet-maker and a coal merchant, respectively.

Following the records through, confirming connections and relationships, still didn't provide much to work with. Both families had common names and I was unable to go back further with any certainty. If you are working on your own tree and encounter these same frustrations, investing in actual certificates is essential – but you still need to prove those connections.

Because I had the children's dates of birth I was able to find William in 1939, married to Lilian Green. The couple lived in Leyton, Essex. William worked in an engineering factory and Lilian assembled electric torch batteries – perhaps working in the Ever Ready factory in nearby Walthamstow.

Lewis's, Liverpool

081330
Mrs S Sweeney
27 Oakleigh Grove
Lower Bebington
Cheshire
Dear Mrs S
We asked Will about your letter. He posted it on his way back. So it was not his fault.
I got home alright on Sat.
Nelly Cooper

Sarah was the daughter of John Preston and she married Samuel Sweeney, a gardener, in 1891. The 1911 census confirms that the couple had two children. Despite Samuel having at least seven siblings their identities weren't easy to confirm. Samuel's parents were James and Mary née Sprout and like Samuel, James was also a gardener.

Although there was little available about the family, I decided to include the Sweeney family in this book for the image – of Lewis's department store in Liverpool. It's such a grand building and must have been quite an attraction. Lewis's was founded in 1856 and was something of a trailblazer with its marketing and central buying practices. The store would be illuminated at night with its tower 'shining like a beacon'. Eventually branches opened in Manchester, Sheffield and Birmingham.

Would Sarah and her family have enjoyed visiting the store? Its location near to Lower Bebington might have allowed them to enjoy window shopping – something not lost on the owners who became known for their creative and eye-catching displays.

Oakleigh Grove is still there – a street of red-brick houses. Some, like number 27, have been rendered and Sarah's house is now a shade of lemon. Although the houses in the road have been extended and modernised, it's still possible to get a sense of the area as it might have been when the Sweeney family were in residence.

I wasn't able to find Nelly – although there were several Nellies. I wonder what was in the letter Will was said to have posted?

Wick Ferry, Christchurch

082261
2 November 1906
Miss E Palmer
Mount Pleasant
Berrow
Near Bridgwater
Dear [Edith]
Just a line to say have not seen anything of the lady.
If I saw anything else should not wait for her. Expect she has someone nearer. It is a quiet time of the year for getting a place just now.
Tell mother received the bacon all right yesterday.
Sorry to hear Mr J is not so well, hoping all all well, as we are.
With much love to all.
From Julia

Edith Palmer (b.1886) was one of 13 children – including sister Julia who was born in 1878. Their parents, Cornelius Palmer and Edith née Toogood were farmers – and both their fathers were also farmers, as were some of their children – but not Julia and Edith.

In 1911, Julia lived in Boscombe, Bournemouth where she worked for her brother, William, who was a baker and confectioner. At this time, he and his wife, Florence née Williams, had left the area and lived in Salcombe, Devon – where their youngest child was born.

In 1901 William and his family lived in Boscombe and Julia is there, working for her brother.

Brothers Ben and Abraham left Somerset for Croydon and worked as a joiner and draper, respectively. Another brother, Albert, worked in Ryde, Isle of Wight as a draper's assistant for a business at 1–2 St Thomas Square. In 1901 he appears in the census returns at that address – along with 15 other assistants. By 1911 he had moved to Croydon and appears in the census return at his brother Ben's address with Abraham.

Larger shops – like Albert's employer – had dormitories where their staff lived 'over the shop'. Female employees were particularly restricted by 'house' rules and were often only allowed away with the permission of their parents.

Edith remained in Somerset and appears in the 1939 register with her husband, Seward Hunt, who was a farm hand.

Buckingham Palace, London

083384
29 May 1911
Mrs Hill
Tritterford Mill
Hall Green, Near Birmingham
36 Aylmer Road
Shepherds Bush, London
Dear Mrs Hill
Just a line to let you know that we are all quite well.
We hope that you have all recovered from your colds by this time and are now in the best of health. I expect your garden is looking very nice now after the nice weather we have had lately. I should very much like to see it. The parks and open spaces here are looking very fine now. Have you started boating on the pool yet?
With sincerest regards to all from my wife and the boys.
Arthur Everall

Although Arthur Rudge Hill and Matilda née Vale had no children that appeared in the records I traced, there were certainly children in their lives. Throughout the census returns appear young nephews and nieces and even an adopted daughter – Emily Louise Knight. She is recorded as both Emily and Louise from 1881 and her year of birth varies from 1873 to 1875. It's not until 1901 that a place of birth is recorded – Redditch, Worcestershire.

Arthur Hill was born in Kings Norton, Worcestershire in 1837 and was the son of Joseph Hill and Phoebe née Rudge. Matilda was born in Haselor, Warwickshire and in 1861, she lived next door to the mill in the card's address (then run by Arthur's father) with her brother John Vale who was a farm bailiff. In later years this house was occupied by others with that same job.

Today, Tritterford (Trittiford) Mill is part of a country park and the mill's pool, which Arthur Everall mentions in his card, is included in a cycle route. Arthur Hill's probate records confirm that he was at the mill until 1916.

Arthur, who sent the card, was born in Kings Norton in 1881 where his father was a foreman in a metal factory. In 1911, in London, Arthur was a clerk in a firm of chartered accountants. By 1939 he was working for Spillers, the food manufacturing company, as head statistical and costings clerk. The company had evacuated from London and the staff relocated to Beechwood House, Hertfordshire. Arthur's wife, Beatrice née Ravenhill, was also born in Kings Norton. In 1939 she lived in Solihull with their youngest child who was born in 1912.

Princetown Prison Gates

084378
26 September 1911
Miss M Carrington
Ermels
Sidegate Lane
Ipswich
Tavistock 25/09/11
I am now going to make my way to this spot but not to stay. It's lovely crossing Dartmoor.
I hope all well.
Best love from Will

May Carrington was born in 1886 in Ipswich, Suffolk and was one of seven children born to William and Mary née Flory. Mary was born in Ipswich but William was born in Thorpe-le-Soken, a small village in Essex, and was a warehouseman working for a tailor.

William junior was a brewer's clerk and Frank worked as a civil servant with the Customs and Excise. William served in the First World War and it's his records that confirm he sent the postcard to May who worked as a draper's assistant – the handwriting being a perfect match.

In 1924 William married Freida née Miller (also recorded as Freda). A year after William's death in 1945, their son William was killed in Palestine where he served with the Information Corps. In June 1946 there were several reports of attacks where soldiers were killed and a Facebook page dedicated to the Information Corps provided the following information about William:

On 17 April 1946 William embarked for the Middle East and arrived in Palestine on 5 May and was sent to Gaza, based at Sarafand. On 16 June, William was returning to Gaza when he came upon an Arab crowd celebrating the escape of the Grand Mufti of Jerusalem to the Middle East.

An accident involving a truck resulted in the vehicle being attacked. William, with great gallantry, went unaided to the driver's assistance and was himself attacked – shot through the head and stabbed. Unconscious, he was rushed to a military hospital where he later died. He is buried at Ramleh War Cemetery, [Ramla] Israel.

The Carrington family had a long relationship with Sidegate Lane beginning with the 1911 census. Probate records from 70 years later confirm that the family remained in either the same house or nearby.

The Capitol, Washington, DC

085281
26 July 1904
Miss Ethel Hall
20 Isabella Street
Old Trafford
Manchester
England
Daddy

In 1901, Ethel lived with her parents, Laurence and Jeannie Hall. Laurence's place of birth is recorded as Canada, in 1861. Ethel and Jeannie were born in Scotland. In 1911 Laurence and Jeannie are at a different address in Manchester and now Laurence's place of birth is in Liverpool. Is it the correct couple?

Earlier, in 1891, the couple were in Scotland with a child, transcribed as Alber. At this time Laurence is again listed as being born in Canada and working as a marine engineer – the same job as in all the other census returns.

Jeannie also proves to be a challenge to pin down. She appears in the trees of other researchers with the maiden name Bowie – she even has a brother named David. But other details don't provide a good means of identifying Jeannie who also went by the name of Jane.

In 1911, Ethel is a boarder in Holyhead, Wales and recorded as Ethel Freda Mosford, music hall performer. With her is William Worth Mosford, her husband of a few months, who was also a performer. Before and after their marriage, the couple performed in variety shows across the UK. In 1909, 'Freda Hardene' was described as 'entertaining' in a review of a show at the Royal Hippodrome, Preston. Other reviews describe her as a 'capable artiste of the society entertainer type'. William was a baritone and they are described in a 1913 review as being 'versatile entertainers, who are a host in themselves'. A review from the Winter Gardens, New Brighton describes William as 'a delightful baritone'. The pages and pages of online reviews covering a number of years confirm the couple were very much a success on the variety circuit.

By 1939, a widow since William's death in 1926, Ethel had moved in with her widowed mother at the 1911 address. Also there in 1939 is James Earley, a theatre manager who worked at the New Hippodrome. Ethel was no longer a performer by this time.

This postcard was such a puzzle. Why would Laurence record his place of birth incorrectly? I almost considered that perhaps there were two families. However, the postcard was sent in 1904 and the family were at that same address when Laurence gave Canada as his place of birth. The handwriting in the 1911 census, where he states Liverpool, matches that on the postcard.

White House, Washington, DC

086279
21 November 1907
Miss Laetitia Millard
C/O Miss Nilson
Duncan House
Clifton
Bristol
England
Cousin A is here in Washington, DC, on business and of course I am here with him. we are well and most comfortable in our hotel – Washington is about 250 miles south of NY – I hope you are well, dear, & enjoying your school. How much we will have to talk about next summer!
Always with love. H.

Even given from where this postcard was sent, it was still surprising to discover the family's trans-Atlantic ancestry.

Florence Laetitia was born in Cheltenham in 1894. Her father was Charles Stuart Millard – a watercolourist who was born in Ontario, Canada. In 1891 he married Florence Oliver who was born in Birkenhead, Cheshire where her father, James, was a shipping agent.

James Oliver's work took him around the world and several of his children were born in Canada. The connection with the Canadian branch of the family was maintained – Florence and Laetitia appear in passenger lists sailing to Canada in the 1920s to stay with Florence's sister, Marion, who was born in Rochester, Kent but had married a Canadian.

Laetitia had at least three brothers (one sibling had died by 1911). Charles served in the First World War and studied medicine. William studied law, and her youngest brother, Lionel, became an actor. In the 1920s he was known for his performances in Shakespearean productions and radio plays. In 1930 he was one of three actors to perform in the first televised play on the BBC. Luigi Pirandello's *The Man with the Flower in his Mouth* was transmitted from the Baird studios in 133 Long Acre, London and the production director was Val Gielgud – brother of Sir John. In 1967 the play was recreated using the same technology and can be viewed online. By 1939, Lionel had become drama advisor for the National Council of Social Service.

Like Charles, Laetitia studied medicine and she eventually had a practice in Harley Street, London. Her probate records show that she lived in Pennsylvania Road, Exeter – a lovely coincidence with the White House (as depicted on the postcard) being in Pennsylvania Avenue.

The Prison, Sark

087283
Grand Hotel
30th January
Mrs Chaplin
7 Devonshire Street
Local
Can you be at the Grand Hotel at 5.45PM Thursday 1st February for a Dinner.
Please reply by return.
A Brunsdon
Waiter

Although the full address wasn't added to the card, the family were found via the cancellation mark in Leicester. Mrs Chaplin – Florence née Bassett (b.1874) – lived in Leicester with her husband Jabez, who was a year younger, and their two surviving children, Doris and Harry. Jabez worked in the shoe-making industry as an engineer's fitter and was one of nine siblings. His father, Mark Chaplin, was a framework knitter.

In 1911, Jabez's mother, Maria née Mason, was a widow and lived with her daughter Clara in Morledge Street, Leicester. I found the death of Mark had been recorded in several trees as being in 1898 in Leicester's workhouse. There was a death certificate confirming that his occupation had been a framework knitter and he had lived in Morledge Street. Clara is given as the person registering the death. No reason is provided as to why he was in the workhouse. The cause of death is given as heart disease.

Jabez's youngest sister, Ada, married Frederick Jackson in 1899 and the couple, with their five children, emigrated to Canada. One document suggests they left in 1922 and mentions that Ada had '£15 in her possession'. A few years later, their daughter Ida married Frank Hale, a caretaker, in Ontario. Frank was originally from Essex. His obituary was published in *The Ottawa Journal* in 1962 and mentions that their children lived in Ottawa and Montreal.

Tracing the sender of the card was relatively straightforward. I searched for a waiter by the name of Brunsdon. Fortunately, Albert (b.1857) was the head of the household in 1911 and completed the census return – allowing me to match his handwriting. His wife, Mary née Gleeson, was born in Carlow, Ireland the same year as her husband. The couple had ten children and by 1911 three had died. Four children were listed in the census – William, Florence, Lilly and Cecil. Those children were born in Edinburgh, Manchester and Canterbury and three of them worked in the shoe industry.

Albert, who sent the postcard, was born in Reading and he appears in several records for military pensions – suggesting that before becoming a waiter in Leicester he was in the army. One document confirmed that he had enlisted when he was 18.

The hotel where Albert and Florence worked is depicted in the next story.

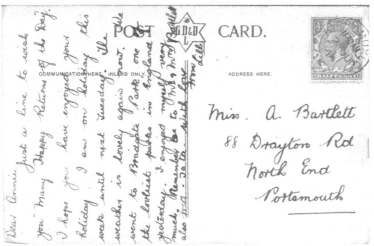

Grand Hotel and King's Hall, Leicester

088295
21 July 1914
Miss A Bartlett
88 Drayton Road
North End
Portsmouth
Dear Annie
Just a line to wish you many Happy Returns of the Day. I hope you have enjoyed your holiday. I am on holiday this week until next Tuesday. The weather is lovely again now. We went to Bradgate Park, one of the loveliest parks in England yesterday. I enjoyed myself very much.
Remember me to Mr and Mrs Bartlett, also Fred. Ta ta.
With love from Lill.

I had high hopes for this postcard – chosen to show the elaborate exterior of Leicester's Grand Hotel – where the recipient and sender of the previous card worked. Unfortunately the information available for Annie Bartlett and her family was sparse.

Annie was born in Portsmouth in 1893. Over the years her father had a number of jobs but at the time the postcard was sent he was employed by the local corporation painting poles for the tramways. Harry Bartlett was born in Fareham, Hampshire and Annie's mother, Sarah née Shorey, was born in Corfe Mullen, Dorset. Although Annie's parents had siblings I wasn't able to confirm with any certainty what happened to them – beyond their names and years of birth. What I do know is that Annie had five siblings and by 1911 two had died. The youngest child I traced was Fred – mentioned in the card. He was at home in 1911 and was a part-time apprentice working in the government docks as a ship fitter.

The Grand Hotel in Leicester opened its doors in 1898 and soon became one of the most prestigious hotels in the area. It even boasted a cinema – The King's Hall Cinema. According to the hotel's current website, Winston Churchill stayed at the hotel in 1909.

Although it's not known when exactly the previous card was sent, it's certainly possible that Albert Brunsdon and Florence Chaplin were working at the hotel at this time. Who knows, perhaps Churchill attended the event Albert was writing to Florence about?

Dear Annie,

I am afraid I am awfully late for the 30th Oct. But I wish you very many happy returns of the day. Yours with Love

Maud

POST CARD

Miss A. Sweeney,
19. Westgate.
Bradford.
Yorkshire.

This Side for England

Liberty Bell, Philadelphia

089266
19 November 1906
Miss A Sweeney
19 Westgate
Bradford
Yorkshire
Dear Annie
I am afraid I am awfully late for the 30th October. But I wish you very many happy returns of the day.
Yours with love
Maud

Annie Sweeney (b.1886) was a printer's stenographer and one of at least eight children born to master jeweller Edward Sweeney and his wife Anne née Peacock. There's no record of Annie marrying and in 1939 she is living with her elder sister Clara who had worked in their father's business with another sister, Mary. Brothers Frank and Edward would become jewellers. Edward and Anne's eldest son, Austin, became a priest.

Several of the siblings appear in online trees as having emigrated to America. However, I couldn't find any documents that supported these instances that could be confirmed back to Edward and Anne. Clearly Annie knew someone who had relocated to America.

Was Maud a friend? I searched the census return for 1901 looking for a Maud who lived nearby. I also searched in America looking for a Maud who lived in Clifton Heights (from where the card was posted) and had been born in Yorkshire. I don't believe she was an aunt – I certainly didn't find a Maud – and a cousin might possibly have been too young (you can just make out that the card was sent in 1906 when Annie was 20). It's a lovely card and you can clearly see the famous crack that was caused, so it is recorded, when the bell was tested.

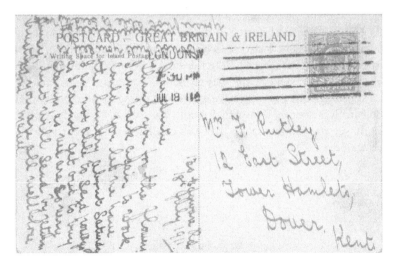

Kew Church

090333
Mrs F Putley
12 East Street
Tower Hamlets
Dover
Kent
130 Edgware Road
18th July 1911
Dear Auntie
Thank you for the flowers.
I am back again to work. Could you let me have the laundry about Saturday. I am not able to send postage as I cannot get out to buy stamps as we are so very busy but will send by return. Trusting you are all well
Love from Mabel

Mabel's auntie was her mother's sister, Sarah Putley née Onn. Sarah lived with her watchmaker husband, Frederick, and was born in Greenwich. Mabel's mother, Louisa, was born in Dover. Their father, Edmund Onn, was in the army and he married their mother, Sarah née Daniel, in Woolwich. After Edmund's death Sarah worked as a storekeeper for a charity in Charlton, Kent. Her father was a coast guard and she was born in the small fishing village of Lulworth in Dorset.

Mabel, who sent the postcard, was the daughter of Louisa and Willie Wollett. In 1911 she was a Church Army mission sister at Edgware Road. Mabel was born in 1887, in Andover, Hampshire. In 1939 she is listed as a Church Army officer in Twickenham with her mother who by this time had been widowed twice. Willie had died when Mabel was a young girl and Louisa later married Henry Watts, another military man.

The Church Army, for whom Mabel worked, was established in 1882 by Wilson Carlile. At the time we know Mabel was in London, they provided support in the form of hostels for those in need. Their website says:

In 1905 more than 350,000 men received temporary residential care in Church Army homes and marquees. There were also a number of new initiatives launched including pioneer tent missions, beach missions, the Church Army Printing Press and the making of cinematic films for evangelism and publicity.

The Army's work continues to this day and helps the most vulnerable in society – the homeless, victims of abuse, any person of any age who needs help.

Chalcombe Church, Bath

091219
2 November 1910
Miss M Wilson Smith
17 Brock Street
Bath

C	*T*	
O	*U*	*O*
N	*L*	*N*
G	*A*	*S*
R	*T*	
A	*I*	
MDC		

Although it can't be confirmed why Marjorie was being congratulated, it could well have been success in an examination. She was born in Bath in 1899 and her parents were Dr Thomas Wilson-Smith (sometimes spelt without a hyphen) and Alice née Wilks. Dr Wilson-Smith was well known in Bath. During the Second World War he opened the Medical Mission, for those who could not afford healthcare.

After school in Bath, Marjorie attended Cheltenham Ladies' College from 1916 to 1918 and I'm indebted to Mrs Rachel Roberts, College Archivist, Cheltenham Ladies' College Archive Service for providing some of the information that follows.

Marjorie left the college to study at the University of London where she achieved a degree in chemistry. Later, she undertook research in chemistry at the Royal College of Science. After her marriage in 1930 she taught practical chemistry at Kings College of Household and Social Science.

Marjorie is mentioned in the book *Chemistry Was Their Life: Pioneering British Women Chemists, 1880–1949* by Marelene F. Rayner-Canham and Geoffrey Rayner-Canham.

From 1921 to 1925, she was a Demonstrator in Chemistry at the London School of Medicine for Women. During this period she was also a research student in the organic chemistry department of Imperial College. Another student was Ernest Farmer – the man she would marry. Before Marjorie's entry, it's mentioned that once married, many of the chemists are 'simply noted as assisting their husbands' and this is, according to the book, true in her case.

Ernest was born in Derbyshire in 1890 and served in the First World War. He sustained life-changing injuries in 1917 that affected his right arm and head and he remained in hospital for almost two years. Although he had trained as a teacher, the effects of his injuries led him to science.

Ernest's career is outlined in *The Chemistry Department at Imperial College London*.

From 1924 he worked on cyclic unsaturated ketones (something that even Google couldn't help me with). One student is recorded as saying that he ran a friendly research group and that they often worked long into the night. Farmer, the student says, was ready to say a humorous word at any time between midnight and dawn and even took his group out to dinner and occasionally to a show. Marjorie was part of this team and worked with him for the rest of his life.

Marjorie kept in touch with her former school and no doubt they were proud of her achievements.

Suffragette Emily Wilding Davison hid in a broom cupboard at the House of Commons. The 1911 census records confirm she was indeed enumerated as a resident there—The National Archives

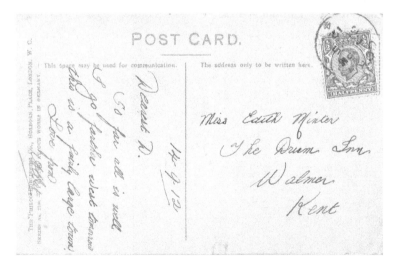

Patrick Street, Cork

092293
14 September 1912
Miss Edith Minter
The Drum Inn
Walmer
Kent
Dearest D
So far all is well. I go farther west tomorrow. This is a fairly large town.
Love from Albert

Edith's family had connections with The Drum Inn back to 1874 and they continued until at least 1956 when her brother, William, is listed in the local telephone directory at the address – the 1939 register records that he ran his private chauffeuring business from there.

Edith was one of nine children and was born in 1905 to William Minter and Edith née Pain – their youngest child of those alive in 1911 (three siblings had died by this time). Edith Pain was born in Deal, Kent in 1873. Her father, Edmund, was a licensed victualler who ran The Lifeboat Inn. Her brother Arthur ran The Saracen's Head, also in Deal.

Although William and Edith remained in the county, other siblings left and settled abroad.

Violet married Canadian George Cushway and the couple eventually moved from Canada to California. In the 1921 Canadian census brother Reginald Minter was living with Violet and her family. He also married a Canadian – Helmi Alitalo (both names appear with different spellings) – and the couple lived in Ontario where Reginald was a mechanic.

Why was the card addressed to 'Dearest D'? Edith's middle name was Jane so that can't be the reason. Could the card have been intended for her mother? That's unlikely because she was also Edith Jane. Although it clearly states 'Miss', it isn't uncommon to see this instead of 'Mrs'.

If the card was intended for Edith, she would have been only seven when she received it. That suggests that the card might be from a relative – perhaps a cousin. Whoever Albert is, Edith kept the card in almost perfect condition. Its glossy finish may have cracked a little but that's typical of cards produced with this finish.

All of the cards I research are chosen at random and I'm always surprised at how many families have members who emigrated to either America or Canada. In this book I'm also surprised that so many of those who emigrated left Kent.

Published, 1906, Standard Pictures Co., Plymouth, Mass.

Pilgrim Memorials, Plymouth and Duxbury

093338
August 1907
Miss Irene M Chandler
30 Bolton Street
Hartland
Maine
ALG

Although using online-only research methods can be limiting, it can also provide a wealth of information that allows you to explore your own ancestry. The postcard sent to Irene Chandler is a lovely example of how records can come together to confirm an identity.

In 1910 she lived with her parents, Howard Chandler and Vilda née Andrews, at Bolton Street. Howard was a superintendent working with electric lights.

In 1920, she lived with her parents and husband and worked as a bookkeeper in a store. She had married Albert George Lord Gearing in 1915. Electrician Albert was born in Canada but became a US citizen in 1917. Might he have sent Irene the card? ALG could be Albert Lord Gearing. By looking at Albert's signature in his First World War records, it's clearly a match. Also, the address given then matches Irene's location in the 1920 census – so we go beyond matching some of Albert's known initials to those on the postcard.

The only question left unanswered is why the postcard was kept. The couple were to divorce and marry new partners. Was the card disposed of and passed around markets and other owners before finding its way to me? The journey of a card can never be fully researched!

Dunster, Market House & Castle

094369
12 January 1911
A Wansbrough-Jones Esq, LLD
'Sherborne'
Attleborough
Norwich
Norfolk
Have received Leek Paper and send sincere condolences. You must have had a trying week.
Am staying here X a few days, and my sister always has a room and welcome for friends
who come this way.
Had a chat with Mr Wood Tuesday – about as usual.
Yours TP

Before I share the story behind this postcard, I have to repeat that when I buy a postcard, all I know is that I can find the recipient in a census return. I never go any further until I have the card in my hand. I chose this particular postcard because it's a familiar view – I've visited Dunster many, many times and even if I don't have time to stop I often drive through on my way to either Minehead or Watchet.

It's clear that the sender of the postcard has a local connection – we know his sister probably lives in the house marked with the X. Over the years the official address of this house has moved from Castle Hill, to the High Street and back to Castle Hill. It might be that I never connect the sender of the card to the correct family. But what of the recipient?

Arthur Wansbrough-Jones was born in Wrexham in 1865. He was a solicitor and the son of Methodist minister John Jones and Mary Ann née Wansbrough. Arthur's names are sometimes hyphenated, sometimes Wansbrough is a middle name, and other times it is part of his surname without a hyphen. Arthur's father was well travelled in his role of minister. In 1851, as a single man, he appears in the census in Paulton, Somerset. Later, with his family, he serves in a number of locations around the country including St Just, Cardiff, Rotherham, Gillingham, Lancaster, Bath, Walsall and Jersey – and those are just the locations that appear in official records.

Arthur attended Kingswood School in Charlcombe, just north of Bath – founded by John Wesley in 1748 to 'provide an education for the sons of Methodist clergymen'.

Arthur's mother, Mary Ann Wansbrough, was born in Bristol in 1829. She was baptised in St Mary's church, Redcliffe. Her parents, John Wansbrough and Jemima née Saunders, were married in the same church in 1818. Mary Ann's baptism records show that the family lived in Guinea Street, Bristol and were still there until at least 1841. If you watched the third series of *A House Through Time*, you might recall that the house researched was number 10 Guinea Street. In 1841, the residents of that house were a couple – William and Ann Harris. Mary Ann and her family lived at number 3. Unlike number 10, this house was demolished and the site forms part of a development of flats.

By 1851, Mary Ann's parents had moved to Old Cleeve, Somerset. Later, they lived at Nettlecombe. When John and Jemima died (1865 and 1862, respectively), they were buried in St Decuman's church, Watchet. By this point in my research, something was tugging at my memory. I have visited Watchet many times and even wandered around this church. The last time was as part of a circular walk created to explore the town's former paper mill and mineral line.

What would eventually become the Wansbrough Paper Mill began in 1750. The paper was known as St Decuman's paper. In 1824, while still in Bristol, John took over the mill with two partners, James Date and William Peach, and gave it its name. John had a Methodist chapel built within the mill's grounds. In 1889 – well after John's death – the mill was damaged by fire. However, the business recovered and was the largest manufacturer of paper bags in the country. The mill, albeit with different owners, continued until 2015. When I completed that circular walk the buildings were still standing, although some parts were being cleared. Almost 200 people were employed at the time of its closure and the effect on the small town was immense.

Other members of the family were involved in the paper business. In 1851, John Wansbrough junior was a wholesale stationer in Bristol. Another son, Henry, moved to Derbyshire where he was a paper-maker's agent.

Back to Arthur – who received the postcard. He married Beatrice Slipper in 1898 and the couple had four children: Harold, Llewelyn, Gwyneth and Owen. All three of the sons had distinguished careers in the military.

Harold served in the Indian army. Llewelyn achieved the rank of Major General. Owen was a researcher into physical chemistry at Cambridge University where he was also a tutor. He eventually became Director of the Special Weapons Unit with the War Office, with the rank of Brigadier and eventually received a knighthood.

Gwyneth graduated from Cambridge University in 1924 and was awarded an OBE in 1967.

Beatrice Slipper, Arthur's wife, was born in Ludham, Norfolk in 1869 and was one of nine children born to Thomas Slipper and Mary née Gooch. Thomas was a landowner and farmer. By 1911 Mary had died and Thomas lived with his daughter, Mary, who was 'manager of house'. A brother, Armine, became a solicitor. A sister, Helen, married the rector of St Mary's church in Attleborough, Norfolk – Maxwell Webb. A window in the church was dedicated to Maxwell in the 1930s. Another sister, Katherine, married Charles Chamberlin, also a vicar, and they lived in Witton. Another brother, Reginald, is listed in 1911 as a grazier in Ludham. We have to go across the

Atlantic to find the three remaining brothers: Thomas, John and Frederick.

In 1901, Thomas is listed as an importer of agricultural implements in Norfolk. In 1907 he married Edith Little and the ceremony was officiated by Charles Chamberlin. Two years later and the couple are recorded as travelling from Canada to Vermont, America. They would eventually settle in Whatcom, Washington State.

John had moved to America in 1885. In 1898 he married Lola Sprinkle in Hamilton, Washington State. Lola was born in Kansas. In 1900, John is listed as a hardware dealer in Hamilton.

In 1902 Frederick married Gertrude Sprinkle – Lola's sister. The 1910 census shows all three brothers living as neighbours in Maple Street, Skagit, Hamilton. Frederick's occupation is given as a merchant in a department store.

The Skagit River Journal (a wonderful online resource) has a detailed history of the Slipper brothers in America written by Noel Bourasaw. The article has an intriguing headline: 'The Slipper brothers help define Hamilton and the Sprinkle sisters tame them'. Attached to the opening section is a wonderful photograph of all nine siblings taken in Norfolk. This excerpt from the article is reproduced by kind permission of the journal:

> *The Slipper family's prominence in Hamilton dates from 1890, right in the middle of the original boom, when financiers promoted the proximity of ore from Coal and Iron mountains across the river… John Slipper soon formed the Eagle Shingle Company somewhere close to the river. That was the umbrella company for various businesses that he and his brother Fred G. would own in town over the next 25 years.*
>
> *By the turn of the century, the Slipper brothers came to the same realization of many early loggers on the river: work in the woods was hard and grueling. Hamilton was growing and needed more retail stores.*
>
> *Around 1900, John moved his Eagle Shingle Company headquarters up to the northwest corner of Maple and Cumberland and started a hardware business, which took off like wildfire. Frederick was his partner and they became substantial members of the community.*
>
> *Over the next few years after 1906, Frederick's general store business thrived and he attained considerable status in town along with brother John.*

The article includes quotes from descendants of the brothers and more wonderful family photos.

When I bought the postcard that began this story, I had no idea where it would lead. From an address in Norfolk, to the West Country and then across the Atlantic.

There is the possibility that the postcard was sent by a school friend of Arthur's. From the 1881 census I found Theodore Piggott – TP – at

Kingswood School with Arthur. He was born in Italy in 1867. Although he had several sisters, I couldn't trace any to Dunster.

Annie Percival provided another red herring – she married William Williams who was a Methodist minister and lived in St Decuman's, Watchet before moving to Dunster. Was William connected to the chapel within the paper mill? With so much research already completed for Arthur's family I've decided not to follow this line – for now...

Why was TP offering his condolences? Arthur's sister Mary was married to solicitor Clement Gwynne and he had died on 1 January 1911 – just a few days before the postcard had been sent. The couple lived in Leek, Staffordshire.

Did you spot any hidden messages on the postcards?

095388

Postscript

Throughout *Posted in the Past – Second Delivery*, I included some of the problems encountered in my research – things that might prepare the beginner genealogist for what lies ahead and to show that problems can be overcome. This short chapter provides more information to help you get started.

The online records available on both sides of the Atlantic cover a lot of the details you need to further your own research. Apart from the usual census returns, records connected with deaths are particularly informative – especially in America. In the UK it's necessary to purchase a death certificate but in America they are often available from the online resource you are using. American certificates include extra information – confirming the names of both parents and their places of birth. The added bonus is the mother's maiden name. With immigration such a big part of America's history it's not surprising to see heritage included in the census returns and other records. In the UK, probate records are incredibly useful in that they often mention the names of the adult children – particularly handy if you're struggling to find a daughter's married name.

I usually purchased a death certificate when the death occurred at a young age. When I was researching the first book, I came across a death that had occurred in a factory. I assumed that this story might lead me to explore health and safety and the conditions of workers. The death certificate gave the cause of death as suicide – and described in graphic detail how this was achieved. This person had served in the First World War and today we are better informed about the effects of conflict on a person's long-term mental health. In the decades that followed the war, many men suffered terribly and perhaps this is what caused my research subject to end his life. Despite knowing, of course, that everyone I've researched is dead, this news – in that detail – was still a shock and he wasn't even my relative. We all know from watching *Who Do You Think You Are?* that the celebrities are often accused of overreacting for the camera and I'm sure in some cases this is true. But when you do discover unsettling facts about your family you are affected and that shock stays with you for a very long time. You also have to consider how and with whom you will share these details.

By this point in the book, you will know how easily errors creep into the records. From transcribers to those completing records, names are misheard and mistakes made. Even when the head of the household has completed their own family details in the 1911 census, you cannot always rely on those details. In my own tree, I was saddened to see that a distant cousin, who created an elaborate tree, had some of my family's names wrong. My father was Arthur John Baggott and he was known to everyone as John. He was recorded in this tree as John. My sister and her children were also incorrectly recorded. I felt that my branch's details were taken from a Christmas card list and this reinforces my own rule – begin with what you *think* you know and then check it. Many family historians regret not being interested enough at a younger age to ask their grandparents questions that would add so much colour to their now hobby of researching their family. Let's take it a stage further – if you are able to ask your parents and grandparents questions, perhaps begin with 'What's your name?'

Looking at my dad's records I found that his Proficiency Certificate, awarded to him in 1948 from Albright Secondary Modern Boys' School in Oldbury, was presented to John Arthur. Later, in 1955, a reference written for him by his first employer referenced Arthur John. Theo Wilkes ran a dairy farm in Inkberrow, Worcestershire and after Dad left agricultural college he worked for Theo and his wife, Betty. I know Dad had fond memories of the family – as do I. Dad and Theo kept in touch and I can remember visiting the family and being impressed with their 'farmhouse kitchen'. I don't know what I was expecting, but it was very nice.

What did surprise me about Dad's reference from Theo was that it was signed CT Wilkes – Cecil Theodore. Even Betty, I discovered, chose to be known by a different name than her official records – Cynthia.

Theo's reference meant a lot to Dad. He kept it in a leather wallet along with other pieces of ephemera. Although I know my father's story, it is still pleasing to know that Theo thought him 'trustworthy and reliable' and that he had 'a large circle of friends' and was a good mixer. He was also a hard-worker and 'a very good milker who maintains his equipment in good order. He takes a genuine interest in all work and is quiet and understanding with the stock in his care'. Years later he put his experience to good use when, at another farm, he finished milking and then delivered me!

Of course, knowing that Dad's school certificate was incorrectly named is a minor detail and possibly something that wouldn't happen today with so much of our details being recorded in computer databases. What is important, to my family, is the memorial to my grandfather, my mother's father. Albert Tatchell was killed in 1953 when the ferry MV *Princess Victoria* was caught in a storm between Stranraer and Larne. The ship's radio officer, David Broadfoot, was posthumously awarded the George Cross for staying at his post until all hope was gone. Captains of merchant ships who attempted to save lives were also recognised. I will always be a supporter of the RNLI for their brave efforts that night. There were only 44 survivors and 135 were lost. The storm fought its way across Scotland and down the east coast of England where it continued to take lives – 531 more would be lost. My grandfather's name appears on memorials at both the ports. A Facebook friend who lives in Stranraer sent me a photo of their memorial and my pleasure at seeing him remembered was diminished with the misspelling of his surname – Tatchel. In Swanage, Tatchell is a local name – rather than common. Mum was born in the town and our family has enjoyed its sea air for generations. I have a greater bond with Swanage than the small village near High Wycombe, Buckinghamshire where I was actually born.

I'm always surprised at how many locations appear in just two generations of my tree. From the south coast of England, to the Midlands and Scotland – and to London where my mum's mother, Violet Abbott, was born – and these are just the milestone locations. How many more are there when you consider relocations for work? And that's important when we research further back. Don't discount a possible breakthrough on your tree just because the location doesn't fit with your assumed heritage.

Rarely during my research did I purchase any certificates. There were some exceptions, but mainly I avoided this. With your own research I would strongly recommend that you consider buying any that move you away from what can already be proven. Online, you will see the marriage registers – and the couple's handwriting – but you may still need the reassurance of birth and death certificates. In America, with more information included in the online documents, you might decide they aren't necessary. I've mentioned how some American families' genealogy is recorded because of their membership of The Sons and Daughters of the American Revolution and connections with the *Mayflower* and American Civil War – and that does help, of course. However, you still need to prove that your branch fits into those trees.

It's estimated there are more than 35 million members of the General Society of Mayflower Descendants. It's no easy process to be accepted into the society. Early in 2020 I attended a talk about the *Mayflower* and the two speakers shared their experiences of joining. One was verified and confirmed, the other was six months into the process. Once the society accepts an application there's still a lot of work needed. Here's what the society's website says:

> *After receiving the results of your Mayflower Lineage Match, you will work with a Member Society historian from one of our 53 Member Societies. All applicants must apply through one of our Member Societies. The Member Society historian will help you determine what documents you need to prove your lineage, and then prepare*

your final application for membership. Your application will then be sent to the General Society of Mayflower Descendants in Plymouth, Massachusetts for verification and approval.

Proving you are descended from a *Mayflower* passenger might not fit with your genealogy goals. You might still be searching for your grandparents' stories. If you use Ancestry, as I do, you will be prompted into reviewing 'hints' and many a good tree has been stumped by accepting these hints without checking. If, for instance, it is suggested that your ancestor had a very specific career, but all your research has led to them being a lowly agricultural labourer, do not accept the information just to enhance your story in the belief someone else has it right – one of you is wrong.

If you are a beginner genealogist, you might have within your family records your parents' marriage and birth certificates. These are the foundations – the roots – of your tree. Beyond those certificates you might have some straggly ideas but you need to focus on the main branches. You will find lots of help and advice online. I subscribe to two magazines (in the UK) – *Family Tree* and *Who Do You Think You Are?* and they never forget that there are those coming to the hobby all the time. As well as articles for those more advanced with their research, there is advice about how to begin the journey. Often you will find special offers for these magazines so you can try a few copies before taking out a longer subscription.

I'd also recommend that you watch, with caution, *Who Do You Think You Are?* and *A House Through Time*. Both are excellent programmes and I look forward to every new episode (and the repeats!). However, they can give a false impression of how easy the research might be. Don't forget that in one episode, they will include research that has taken days, weeks and even months. What they do convey is the wonderful results of that research – and how exciting it is to make those discoveries. Of course, *A House Through Time* explores many families – through the life of one house – and this is another aspect you can bring to your own research. Who lived in your house? In the UK, the 1939 register is probably the best and easiest starting point. You could also consider 'a one place study'. The society has a website and they welcome new enquiries: www.one-place-studies.org.

I'm often asked why I began researching other people's trees. I know I've explained the story of Gilbert Freeman and his family, and how I decided to explore Gilbert's short life, but what about the others? Well, I strongly believe that all these trees are connected. The milliner, draper's assistant, surgeon, sailor, soldier could all be our ancestors. Their experiences – of war, illness, living conditions – would certainly be common to many. Learning about other families allows us to learn about our own.

When I research families in the UK I know that they were all affected by the First World War – even if the family didn't reveal a soldier. It was no different in America. With the cards chosen at random I was struck by how many had direct connections with the Civil War. In genealogy terms it wasn't that long ago and although not in living memory, you don't have to go far back to find the grandchildren who would have heard grandpa talk (or more likely, not talk) about the war. Those dreadful experiences mirror those of any conflict. Often someone only discovers about the heroics of a relative through their military records. In some ways it's a disappointment that those memories weren't shared, but the people concerned were likely protecting their family from the realities they endured and the memories would have been painful to recall.

There is so much to discover about our pasts and the records we can access are increasing all the time. Local family history groups have volunteers that transcribe records and this information is shared online. Even if you live away from the area of your research, your local branch will still be able to help. Groups book speakers on a variety of topics and if you're interested in learning about your ancestors in general terms, this is an entertaining way to do so.

Posted in the Past has become more than a writing project to me. Exploring the families I've researched has led me to discover more about my own. *Second Delivery* has been rewarding in that I've now learned more about America's history – from the tragedy of war to new enterprises. The next book in the series, *Hands Across the Sea*, will focus on travel – of emigration, holidays and the search for work. From messages that tell of stormy weather, of 'nearly being blown overboard' to the sadness of leaving home for something quite unknown – each card has its own story and I begin with that of the *Titanic*.

And remember, *take great care of these people, their lives were as precious to them as yours is to you.*

Index of Names & Locations

Posted in the Past
Hands Across the Sea
Revealing the true stories of day trips, holidays and emigration

I am a stranger in a strange land. My large trunks have not turned up. The US customs took my brandy from me. I am wet through. I have had a poisoned finger. Love to you both.

It is that rough you cannot keep on your feet. Rained every day since we came. I hope to goodness it will be better before we come back. Were nearly tossed off the boat coming. I think I shall be washed overboard.

Just to let you know that I am still alive and haven't been sick much. We are off the coast of Newfoundland. It ain't half rocking.

Coming soon…

About the Author

Helen Baggott grew up in Swanage. Although she no longer lives in the seaside town, Dorset is still home.

For as long as she can remember, she has always loved history and writing – one of her first pieces of non-fiction was a project about the Outer Hebrides island of St Kilda. Although she was only 12 years old, she dreamed that researching and writing would be a major part of her future life.

She has written for local magazines including *Dorset Life* and magazines whose readers enjoy collecting postcards. Helen combines writing with her role as a freelance copy-editor.

The *Posted in the Past* series has, says Helen, given her the perfect excuse to buy more postcards…

Contact Helen by email: PostedInThePast@gmail.com
Facebook and Twitter: @PostedInThePast
View the postcards mentioned in this book in colour:
PostedInThePast.blogspot.com

Made in the USA
Middletown, DE
18 June 2021